MW01142324

ENJOYING THE RICHES OF CHRIST FOR THE BUILDING UP OF THE CHURCH AS THE BODY OF CHRIST

WITNESS LEE

Living Stream Ministry
Anaheim, CA

First Edition, April 2000.

ISBN 0-7363-0883-0

Published by

Living Stream Ministry
2431 W. La Palma Ave., Anaheim, CA 92801 U.S.A.
P. O. Box 2121, Anaheim, CA 92814 U.S.A.

Printed in the United States of America

00 01 02 03 04 05 / 9 8 7 6 5 4 3 2 1

CONTENTS

PREFACE

This book is composed of messages given by Brother Witness Lee in Chicago, Illinois in August and September of 1971. These messages were not reviewed by the speaker.

CHAPTER ONE

GOD'S ETERNAL PURPOSE
TO PRODUCE THE CHURCH

Scripture Reading: Eph. 1:5, 9, 17-23; 2:15; 3:8-11; 4:11-12

GOD'S PURPOSE, WILL, AND GOOD PLEASURE

The eternal purpose of God mentioned in Ephesians 3:11 is the purpose God made in and for eternity. This purpose is something of God's good pleasure and will (1:5, 9). These three things are related: purpose, good pleasure, and will.

Ephesians 1:9 speaks of "the mystery of His will." God's will is a mystery because from the beginning of the world God did not reveal His pleasure to anyone. It was something hidden in God. Although today we have the Bible, many people still do not know the purpose of the universe. Why was the universe created with the heavens, the earth, and billions of creatures? Why was man created? What is the purpose of man's creation? These questions have puzzled many great men. Throughout time, many strong, clever, and thoughtful men have been puzzled by such questions and have tried in vain to discover the purpose of the universe. Some may say that the purpose of creation with all the beauty of nature is to glorify God. Apparently, this answer is good, but it is merely something that we have inherited from the Christian religion; it comes short of revealing what God's purpose is according to the book of Ephesians.

GOD'S PURPOSE BEING TO HAVE THE CHURCH

God's purpose is to have the church. Genesis 1 reveals that God created the heavens and the earth with billions of items. God then created man as the center of His creation

(vv. 26-27). God's intention in creating billions of items with man as the center is to have the church. Without the heavens and the earth, man cannot exist, yet man's existence is for the church. This is according to God's plan, God's purpose. Ephesians 3:10-11 says, "In order that now to the rulers and the authorities in the heavenlies the multifarious wisdom of God might be made known through the church, according to the eternal purpose which He made in Christ Jesus our Lord." *Eternal purpose* can be translated "eternal plan." God planned in eternity and for eternity to have the church.

God planned to have the church because this is His good pleasure. We may compare this to eating dessert; we eat dessert because it is our pleasure to do so. The good pleasure of God's will is to have the church. Many Christians talk about the will of God, yet few know what the will of God is. The will of God is to have the church. God has only one will. Our marriage and our education must be a part of this will. If our marriage and education are a part of the church, then they are something in God's will. If they are not a part of the church, although we may consider them to be in God's will, in reality they are not. To repeat, God has only one will, which is the church.

God has a plan, and this plan was made according to the pleasure of His will. In past ages this plan was a mystery, but today this plan is no longer a mystery; it is a revelation. God's will is the church. God's purpose and plan are the church. God's good pleasure is the church. The book of Ephesians clearly reveals that the church is God's will, His plan, and His good pleasure. I was in Christianity for many years, but I did not see this. Hallelujah, now we have seen this, and today we are in it! We need to always be under His enlightenment, from morning to evening, day and night, today and unto eternity, to see that God's plan, His purpose, His will, and His good pleasure are to have the church. If we care for the church, then our marriage, education, job, and future will all be covered.

Some people have condemned me for being too much for the church. We all should be "too much" for the church. We care for the church because God cares only for the church. God dreams about the church and desires to have the church. He has no desire for anything else. Strictly speaking, God is not interested in our marriage, education, job, health, family, husband, wife, children, or parents. God is interested in the church.

THE CROSS OF CHRIST
PRODUCING THE ONE NEW MAN

The church was produced by Christ on the cross (Eph. 2:15). On the negative side, Christ abolished all the ordinances on the cross, and on the positive side, He created one new man of two peoples, the Jews and the Gentiles. Today this one new man is the Body of Christ, the church. The old man was created, and the new man, the church, was also created. The church, the new man, was created by Christ in Himself on the cross. We know that Christ died on the cross for our sins, yet few have heard that Christ died on the cross to create the one new man, the church. This shows that the cross of Christ is very great.

God created a corporate man and called their name Adam (Gen. 5:1-2). God's intention in creating this corporate man was to express Himself. However, this corporate man failed God and was divided through the fall by all kinds of ordinances. These ordinances are all the different ways of living. The Jews, the Gentiles, the Americans, the British, the French, the Japanese, the Chinese, the Filipinos, the Puerto Ricans, the Yankees, and the Texans each have their own way of living. Men, women, the older generation, and the younger generation also have their own way of living. These ways of living are the ordinances, and these ordinances are used by the subtle enemy to divide humanity.

The old man failed God, but God's intention was to create a new man. On the cross, Christ eliminated all the different ordinances. He also eliminated all the different peoples. All the Americans, British, Chinese, Japanese, Yankees, Texans, and Californians have been crucified. Christ not only crucified the old things and the negative things, but He also created something new—the one new man, the church.

THE ALL-INCLUSIVE DEATH OF CHRIST
PRODUCING THE ONE NEW MAN

The death of Christ on the cross was all-inclusive. Not only did man die there, but God also died there. God died on the cross in order to be released. John 12:24 says, "Unless the grain of wheat falls into the ground and dies, it abides alone; but if it dies, it bears much fruit." When the grain falls into the earth and dies underneath the earth, it grows up and is released to become many grains. God in Christ died on the cross. Death, however, can never terminate God, just as death does not terminate a grain of wheat. Seeds are not afraid of death; they expect to be put into death. To put a seed into death affords it the best opportunity to be released. The reason for this is that there is life within the seed. We as human beings are afraid of death because if we are put into death we are terminated. However, God is life. God is not afraid of death. God went into death and Hades and had a tour of death. He walked into death and walked out. Death cannot hold Him, the resurrection life (John 11:25). God went into death, and death could not hold Him. Rather, it helped Him to be released.

Our wonderful Jesus is God and man; He is a God-man. When He died on the cross, both God and man died there. God died there to be released, and man died there to be terminated. The cross was a termination to man and a release to God. Whatever you are, whatever I am, whatever the Jews are, and whatever the Gentiles are were terminated on the cross. Whether or not we believe this, it is still the fact. Even before we were born, we all were terminated on the cross. It is not a small thing that Jesus died on the cross, because when Jesus died, God died in Him and man died in Him.

In the death of Christ the old man was terminated and God was released. In this release the one new man was produced. Christ's all-inclusive death accomplished a mingling. By the death of Christ we can now be one with God. By the incarnation of Jesus, God came into man, but by the death and resurrection of Christ, man has been brought into God. On the cross man was terminated, while in resurrection man was brought into the release of God. This release produced the one new man. Regardless of whether or not we know this or believe it, it is a fact. The angels know it, the demons know it, and Satan knows it even more. The church was produced by the all-inclusive death of Christ.

THE POWER WROUGHT IN CHRIST
PRODUCING THE CHURCH

God is too great; He is unlimited. We count time by days, but God does not. To Him a thousand years are like one day (2 Pet. 3:8), and one day is like a few moments. God created the universe, and then He accomplished an all-inclusive death on the cross, producing the church. God was happy, but He still had to do something in time. Therefore, God sounded out the gospel to the whole earth. We heard the gospel and believed. Many Christians cannot explain why they believed, but once they believed, they could not give up their faith. I myself tried to forget about Jesus, but I never could do it. Some people say that to believe is just a superstition, but we cannot help believing.

This believing ability is the power of Christ applied to us. Ephesians 1:19-22 speaks of the surpassing greatness of His power, "which He caused to operate in Christ in raising Him from the dead and seating Him at His right hand in the heavenlies, far above all rule and authority and power and lordship and every name that is named not only in this age but also in that which is to come; and He subjected all things under His feet and gave Him to be Head over all things to the church." These verses reveal a fourfold power: resurrecting power, transcending power, subduing power, and overruling power. All this power is to the church.

When we believed in Jesus, we were joyful and peaceful, but much more than this, a kind of power was transmitted into us. Why did we believe? It is because a power was transmitted into us. We could not escape. We may say that our believing into Christ made us happy, but even if we were weeping, we would still have to believe into Him because a kind of power came into us. This is the power that resurrected Christ from the dead, the power that raised Him to the heavenlies, the power that subjected all things under His feet, and the power that made Christ Head over all things to the church. This is why, in a sense, our believing in Jesus does not depend on us. Some of the young ones may want to give up, at least in part, but this does not depend on them; God will never give up A power from on high is constantly transmitting Him into us.

This power is not merely to save us from God's judgment and hell. According to Ephesians, this power is to make us a living part of the church, the Body of Christ, the fullness of the One who fills all in all. We do not have to worry about eternal perdition. Because we are a part of the Body of Christ, God will never send us to the lake of fire. He will surely put His Body in the proper place. Therefore, we should be at peace, forget about heaven and hell, and focus on the church. The power which was wrought in Christ is being transmitted to us to make us a living part of the church. This is on one side.

On the other side, however, we must cooperate by removing any insulation which hinders the transmission of this power. The flow of electricity can be frustrated by even a little insulation. The power that was wrought in Christ is being transmitted to us, yet many times there is insulation within us. This is the reason that the power wrought in Christ does not seem to be very powerful in us. We must condemn this insulation and repent of it by making a confession, applying the blood to cleanse and wash away the insulation. If we do this, immediately we will have the sensation of something flowing within us. This is the current of the heavenly electricity. Then we will sense that we are under the empowering and that we are in the church and for the church.

ENJOYING THE RICHES OF CHRIST
TO BECOME THE FULLNESS OF CHRIST

The power of Christ is one thing, but the riches of Christ are another. We not only must experience the power of Christ; we also must enjoy all the riches of Christ (Eph. 3:8). It is not only a matter of confessing our failures, repenting of our insulation, and applying the blood for all the negative things. We also have to learn how to enjoy the riches of Christ. Many people today have five or six meals a day, including breakfast, lunch, and dinner with a morning, afternoon, and evening snack. Even just to drink something is to take in nutrients. In the same way that we enjoy the riches of food day by day, we must enjoy the riches of Christ. We need to experience the heavenly power, the heavenly electricity, but if we do not enjoy the riches, we will be empty and hungry. Regardless of how much power we experience, we still need to enjoy the riches of Christ.

Ephesians 3 shows us that the church comes out of the enjoyment of the riches of Christ. In verses 8 and 9 Paul announces to the Gentiles the unsearchable riches of Christ as the gospel and enlightens all that they may see what the economy of the mystery is. Then in verse 10 the multifarious wisdom of God is made known through the church. The church comes out of the enjoyment, the dispensing, of the riches of Christ. The riches of Christ include life, wisdom, light, power, love, patience, and humility. Whatever we need, Christ is. He is everything. When we enjoy the riches of Christ, they are dispensed into us.

The best way to enjoy the riches of Christ is to pray-read the word of God. All the riches of Christ are on every page, line, sentence, and word of the Bible. We should not merely exercise our mind to read and understand; this is the wrong way. Rather, we must learn to pray-read. The food on a dining table is for eating, not for understanding. When we come to the Bible, we should not try only to understand it. The Bible is not merely to understand; it is mainly for eating. Jeremiah 15:16 says, "Your words were found and I ate them, / And Your word became to me / The gladness and joy of my heart." In Matthew 4:4 the Lord Jesus also said, "Man shall not live on bread alone, but on every word that proceeds out through the mouth of God." By these verses we can realize that the Bible is a book for us to eat. When we eat the word of God, we enjoy the riches of Christ. Ephesians 6:17-18 says that we must take the word of God by means of all prayer. To take the word of God by means of all prayer is to pray-read.

We must enjoy the riches of Christ, not only the power wrought in Christ. There is a difference between the riches of

Christ and the power of Christ. If our spouse or roommate gives us a difficult time and causes us to become angry, we need power to overcome our temper. Just by calling on the name of the Lord we receive the power of Christ, which is like electricity transmitted to us. However, this is only one aspect. Another aspect is our enjoyment of Christ throughout the day, when the times are good. It is not that we only experience power when we have a difficult time, but that we take the Lord by eating the word daily, at least three or four times a day. We must learn to eat the Lord day by day. Through pray-reading the word of God we enjoy Christ.

When we experience the power and enjoy the riches of Christ, we are the proper church. The church is not merely a group of Christians. The church is Christ as power experienced by the saints and Christ as riches enjoyed by the saints. The more we are in His power and participate in His riches, the more we become the church, His Body, His fullness (Eph. 1:22-23).

THE GIFTED PERSONS BEING GIVEN TO THE BODY BY THE HEAD FOR THE BUILDING UP OF THE BODY

The apostles, prophets, evangelists, and shepherds and teachers are given by the Head to build up the Body (Eph. 4:11-12). This is different from today's Christianity where many gifted persons are merely doing a work. The gifted persons were given to build up the Body.

We should pray-read the verses in this message until we enter into the truth and experience of the purpose of God; the cross of Christ, which produced the new man; the power wrought in Christ, which is transmitted to us that we may be the church; the riches of Christ for our enjoyment that we may be the fullness of Christ; and the gifted persons, who are given to the Body by the Head for the building up of the Body. Regardless of what the situation is in Christianity, we must be clear that God's purpose is to have the Body of Christ, the church, as the fullness of Christ and the new man.

CHAPTER TWO

THE ECONOMY OF THE MYSTERY
FOR THE DISPENSING OF CHRIST

Scripture Reading: Eph. 3:8-10; Col. 1:15-18; Isa. 9:6; Matt.
16:16-18; 1 Cor. 15:45b; 2 Cor. 3:17; Col. 3:4a, 10-11; 2:6; 1 Cor.
6:17

CHRIST BEING MYSTERIOUS AND INCOMPREHENSIBLE

The source of the church is Christ; the church comes out of
Christ. But who is Christ and what is Christ? Christianity
has tried to teach clearly about Christ. Today even a young
believer can say something definite about Christ. Yet the
more we study the Bible, the more we realize that it is difficult to completely comprehend who and what Christ is. It is
easy to understand many other things, but it is very difficult
to know Christ completely. Many in Christianity think that
they know Christ in a complete way, but in actuality, there is
no possibility to completely know Christ. He is too wonderful,
too all-inclusive, too mysterious, and too marvelous.

Even we as men are mysterious. We have three lives: a
physical life, a soulish life, and a spiritual life. Yet we do not
know ourselves completely. How then can we completely comprehend Christ? We have a mind and emotion, but where is
our mind, and where is our emotion? We have two hearts: a
physical heart and a psychological heart. Medical doctors can
touch our physical heart, but they cannot touch our psychological heart. We also have a soul and a spirit, but where is our
soul, and where is our spirit? I know much about myself, but I
am not completely clear about myself. I know that I have a
mind, an emotion, and a will; I know that I have two hearts;
I know that I have a soul and a spirit; and I know that I have

a physical life, a soulish life, and a spiritual life. I have so many good things, but I am not so clear about all these things. We are wonderful, but we are not as wonderful as Christ is. Christ is much bigger than we are; He is all-inclusive. Forty years ago I thought I was very clear about Christ, but today, if you ask me about Christ, I must confess that although I know much about Him, I am not very clear about Him. It is not possible to completely comprehend all the things concerning Christ. Therefore, I have no intention of trying to make you clear. Rather, I may puzzle you. If we are going to enjoy Christ, we have to be puzzled. When we are clear about Christ, we are finished with the enjoyment of Christ. Therefore, it is better not to be so clear.

CHRIST BEING GOD AND THE IMAGE OF GOD

John 1:1 says, "In the beginning was the Word, and the Word was with God, and the Word was God." According to this verse, Christ is God. This point is very clear. Colossians 1:15 says that Christ is "the image of the invisible God." Is Christ God or the image of God? Since God is invisible, how can He have an image? Does anything invisible have an image? To be sure, an image must be visible. As God, Christ is invisible, yet He is the image of the invisible God. This is a puzzle to our mind.

CHRIST BEING THE FIRSTBORN OF ALL CREATION

The latter part of Colossians 1:15 says that Christ is the Firstborn of all creation. This indicates that He is one among the creatures. He is the Firstborn, the first item, of all creatures. Then verse 16 says that "in Him all things were created." This means that He is also the Creator. Is Christ the Creator or a creature? To be sure, He is the Creator, but He is also an item of creation. I have composed several hymns on the subject of Christ being the creature as well as the Creator. Some have condemned me for teaching this, but I do not care whether or not they condemn me. Rather, I care for Colossians 1:15b, which says that Christ is the Firstborn of all creation. Our Lord Jesus Christ is too wonderful. He is not only the

Creator, He is also the creature, and He is not only God, He is also man.

If we recognize that Christ is a man, we have to admit that He is a creature, because man is a creature. Christ partook of blood and flesh (Heb. 2:14), and blood and flesh are items of creation. The so-called systematic theology says that Christ is the Creator and admits that Christ became a man, but it is reluctant to admit that Christ is also a creature. However, as man is Christ not a creature? How could He have blood and flesh without becoming a creature? He is the Creator, yet one day He became a man, a creature with blood and flesh.

CHRIST BEING THE FIRSTBORN FROM THE DEAD

Colossians 1:18 reveals that Christ is the Firstborn from the dead. He is the Firstborn of all creation, and He is also the Firstborn of all the resurrected ones. According to this verse, He is also the Head of the Body, the church. Christ is so many things.

CHRIST BEING THE FATHER, THE SON, AND THE SPIRIT

Isaiah 9:6 is a puzzling verse, containing many points which no theologian can reconcile. It says, "For a child is born to us, / A son is given to us; / And the government / Is upon His shoulder; / And His name will be called / Wonderful Counselor, / Mighty God, / Eternal Father, / Prince of Peace." According to this verse, the child is the Mighty God and the son is the Eternal Father. Is Christ the Son or the Father?

God is triune—the Father, the Son, and the Spirit. Yet Isaiah 9:6 says that the Son is the Father. Furthermore, according to 1 Corinthians 15:45b, Christ as the last Adam became a life-giving Spirit. This is confirmed by 2 Corinthians 3:17 which says, "And the Lord is the Spirit." In this verse the Lord is Jesus Christ (4:5). Hence, the Lord Jesus Christ is the Spirit. Is Christ the Son, the Father, or the Spirit? Eventually, we have to say that He is everything.

CHRIST BEING ALL-INCLUSIVE

Many verses in the New Testament show us that Christ is a man (1 Tim. 2:5; John 1:14; 4:29; 19:5; Acts 2:22; Rom. 5:15).

Is He man or God? He is both; He is everything. He is God, He is man, He is the Father, He is the Son, He is the Spirit, He is the Creator, and He is also the creature. He is the Firstborn, and He is the last Adam. He is the First and the Last, the Alpha and the Omega (Rev. 22:13). He is not the first and the last only, He is also the second, the third, the fourth, and every letter. He is the Alpha, the Beta, the Gamma, and ultimately He is the Omega. He is everyone and He is everything (Col. 3:11). According to systematic theology, Christ is the Son only, but the Bible tells us that He is not only the Son, but also the Father and the Spirit. Based upon this word some may think that I am for the "Jesus only" theology. No, I do not care for any theology; I only care for the pure word of the Bible. We must forget all the theologies and teachings that we picked up from Christianity and come back to the pure Word.

In John 14 Philip asked the Lord Jesus to show him the Father. The Lord Jesus rebuked him by saying, "Have I been so long a time with you, and you have not known Me, Philip? He who has seen Me has seen the Father; how is it that you say, Show us the Father?" (vv. 8-9). In such a word the Lord seemed to say, "I have been with you for three and a half years. Don't you know Me? Haven't you seen Me? If you have seen Me, why do you ask Me to show you the Father? Don't you know that if you have seen Me, you have seen the Father?"

The Lord Jesus is wonderful and all-inclusive. He is all in all. Is there God in this universe? Yes, but without Christ and outside of Christ we cannot find God. God is in Christ, and Christ is God. Is there a real man in this universe? Yes, this real man is Christ. Is there a heavenly Father? Yes, He is Christ. Is there the Son of God? Yes, He is Christ. Is there the Spirit of God? Yes, He is Christ. If we say that Christ is the Son and not the Father or the Spirit, then we cannot say that Christ is all. Yet Christ is all and in all. He is God, He is the Father, He is the Son, He is the Spirit, He is a man, and He is the life. He is everything.

Eventually, Christ is even you and me. Philippians 1:21 says, "For to me, to live is Christ," and Galatians 2:20 says, "I am crucified with Christ; and it is no longer I who live, but it is Christ who lives in me; and the life which I now live in the flesh I live in faith, the faith in the Son of God, who loved me and gave Himself up for me." This verse is very puzzling. First, it says that "I am crucified with Christ"; this means that I am brought to an end. Then it says, "It is no longer I who live, but it is Christ who lives in me," yet "I live in faith." This indicates that, spiritually, Christ has become us. Christ is not only the Head but also the Body (Col. 1:18; 1 Cor. 12:12). Christ is everything.

CHRIST BEING IN US AS OUR LIFE

The all-inclusive Christ, the very Christ who is all and in all, is our life (Col. 3:4). Today He is in us, for He cannot be our life without being in us. Some say that Christ is only in the heavens, yet they also say that Christ is their life. How can this be? How could Christ be our life when He is only in the heavens and we are on the earth? This would mean that our life is in the heavens far away from us. This so-called systematic theology is too systematic. Praise the Lord, the Christ who is our life is not only in the heavens! He is also in us, and He is one with us, as 1 Corinthians 6:17 says: "But he who is joined to the Lord is one spirit."

THE ECONOMY OF THE MYSTERY

Ephesians 3:8 and 9 says, "To me, less than the least of all saints, was this grace given to announce to the Gentiles the unsearchable riches of Christ as the gospel and to enlighten all that they may see what the economy of the mystery is, which throughout the ages has been hidden in God, who created all things." The economy of the mystery in verse 9 is the dispensing of the unsearchable riches of Christ in verse 8.

The Steps of God's Economy

Creation

For God to dispense His unsearchable riches is not an easy or simple thing. God's economy is not first a matter of preaching the gospel. The first matter in God's economy is creation. In creation God brought all things, especially man, into being.

In order for Christ to be dispensed into us, we first needed to
be created. If we were never created, how could Christ be dispensed into us? Thank God for His creation! Creation is the
first step of God's economy.

Incarnation

After creation, the next step in God's economy is incarnation. Creation is to bring man into existence, while incarnation
is to bring God into man, into His creation. Before incarnation, God was God and man was man; these two were
separate. Through incarnation, however, God came into man.
The issue was a man named Jesus, who was not only man but
also God. He is man and God, God with man; therefore, His
name is Emmanuel, which means God with us (Matt. 1:23).

Crucifixion

Incarnation brought God into man, but God's economy was
still not complete. After incarnation comes crucifixion. Creation brought us into being, incarnation brought God into us,
and crucifixion terminates us. First, Christ brought God into
us, then in crucifixion, He brought us to the cross and terminated us (Gal. 2:20; Rom. 6:6).

Resurrection

The next step is resurrection. Resurrection is to bring us
into God. Incarnation brings God into us, and resurrection
brings us into God. These steps of creation, incarnation, crucifixion, and resurrection are the economy of the mystery.
Today this economy is still a mystery to many people, but
today we know this economy, this dispensation, of such a
wonderful Christ.

Ascension and Descension

After resurrection is ascension. Ascension is to bring man
to the throne. Then following ascension is descension. Descension is the coming down of the Spirit on the day of Pentecost
(Acts 2:1-4). What is the work of the Lord as the Spirit today?
It is to bring Christ, the Head, into His Body. How much we
are built up depends upon how much Christ is wrought into

us as the Head. This is the meaning of descension. Today, it is altogether a matter of working Christ into us in His descension.

Christ's Second Coming

God needs all the foregoing steps, but this is not yet the end. The end of the steps is Christ's second coming, the time of the rapture. At this time Christ will be fully wrought into His Body, not in all of His believers, but at least in a group of overcomers. Christ as the Head will be wrought into this group of overcomers, and these overcomers will be the bride ready for His coming (Rev. 19:7).

Christ Bringing the Head into the Body

We may feel that the preaching of the gospel is to make people happy and peaceful. To Christ, however, the preaching of the gospel is to bring the Head into people. As I share Christ with you, I am bringing the Head into you. Now after Pentecost, the Lord Himself as the Spirit—the Spirit of life and the Spirit of power—is constantly working on us to bring Himself as the Head into His Body, that is, to work Himself into us. Salvation is not merely for salvation; salvation is to bring the Head into the Body. Growth in life is not merely for the growth in life; it is to bring the Head more and more into the Body. To overcome our temper is also not merely to overcome our temper; this means very little. To overcome our temper is to bring Christ as the Head into the Body.

Today we Christians may not have this concept. We are too religious, too natural, too personal, and too selfish. We may think salvation is something only for us and that to overcome our temper and the world and to be spiritual, holy, divine, and heavenly are a personal matter. Yet all these things are for bringing the Head into the Body. If we care for bringing the Head into the Body, we will be in the heavens. If we care for this, our temper and even the world will mean nothing to us, but if we do not care for bringing the Head into the Body and only care for victory over the world, we will have a difficult job. The more we try to overcome the world, the more the world will overcome us. Likewise, if we are only for brotherly love, we will never have brotherly love. Brotherly love is for the Head to be brought into the Body. Today everything is for bringing the Head into the Body. All the gifts, including the apostles, the prophets, the evangelists, and the shepherds and teachers, are for bringing the Head into the Body. Whatever work we do and whatever we are should be for bringing the Head into the Body. If by our receiving these messages the Head works Himself more into us, that is wonderful; otherwise, these messages are in vain.

THE REVELATION OF CHRIST AND THE VISION OF THE CHURCH

It is truly difficult to say who Christ is and what Christ is because He is too wonderful and all-inclusive. He is too much for us to comprehend. Many verses are required to make known who Christ is. What I have spoken here is not my own teaching. I am simply opening up the verses concerning Christ.

The church comes out of Christ's dispensing. In the Bible both the revelation concerning Christ and the vision concerning the church are marvelous. We can never exhaust the understanding of these two items. Because many of us have been frustrated and distracted by old teachings, it is better for us to forget all these teachings. We may have thought that we knew the church and that we knew Christ. Whenever someone spoke about Christ or whenever we heard the term *church,* we may have said, "I know that. I know Matthew 16:16 and 18." Actually, we did not know very much.

A BRIEF SUMMARY OF THE ECONOMY OF GOD

May the Lord be merciful to us to bring us back to the proper understanding of His economy and the realization that we need the dispensing of Christ. God's creation is to bring us into being, incarnation is to bring God into us, crucifixion is to terminate us, resurrection is to bring us into God, ascension is to bring the Body into the Head, and descension is to bring the Head into the Body. When Christ ascended into the heavens, He brought all of us into the heavens (Eph. 4:8). In this way He brought all of us into the headship of Christ. After ascension, He came down to bring the Head into the Body.

We thank God that He accomplished creation so that we have existence. We are what we are by God's creation. We thank God that He also accomplished incarnation to bring Himself into us. Then He accomplished crucifixion, not only dealing with sins and the world, but also terminating us. After this, in resurrection He brought us into Himself. Then in ascension He brought all the members of His Body into His headship. Hence, we all are in the heavenlies with the Head (2:6). Then after His ascension, He came down as the life-giving Spirit. Now He is working to bring Himself as the Head into us, that is, to bring the Head into the Body. This is the real building up of the Body.

When we preach the gospel, we bring the Head into sinners. When we edify the saints, we bring more and more of the Head into the Body. Whatever we do today must be for the dispensing of Christ as the Head into all His members. Then, at the fullness of times, at least a part of the Body will be ready, mature, and ripe—good for being taken up. This will be the rapture, the day of the wedding of the Lamb. Now we are not only waiting for that day, we are passing through a process under the dispensing of Christ. This is God's economy. God's desire is that all men see what the economy of the mystery is (3:9). Now we are under the dispensing of Christ. God is daily and hourly dispensing all the unsearchable riches of Christ into us.

LEARNING TO WALK IN CHRIST
BY WALKING IN OUR SPIRIT

This dispensing is altogether a matter in the spirit. This wonderful, all-inclusive Christ is the life-giving Spirit (1 Cor. 15:45b), and today this life-giving Spirit is in our spirit. "He who is joined to the Lord is one spirit" (1 Cor. 6:17). Now we all have to learn how to walk in Him. Colossians 2:6 says, "As therefore you have received the Christ, Jesus the Lord, walk in Him." He is not in the heavens only as many in Christianity teach. If He were only in the heavens, how could we walk in Him on earth? Today He is the life-giving Spirit who is one with our spirit. Now we must walk in Him. To walk in Him is simply to behave ourselves in our spirit. We must not care for our emotions, our mind, or our will. We must simply care for our spirit and walk in the spirit. Because He is one with us in our spirit, as long as we walk in the spirit, we are walking in Him. If as young persons we have something to say to our parents, yet in our spirit we sense that it is negative, we must not say it. If we have the desire to go fishing or to go dancing, yet in our spirit we sense something negative, we should not go. We must simply take care of our spirit. There is only one way today, which is to walk in Christ who is the Spirit in our spirit. To walk in Christ simply means to walk in our spirit. In this spirit we are one with Him. It is by this kind of walk that His day-by-day and hour-by-hour dispensing of Himself into us takes place. Then the church comes out of such a dispensing. This is the proper church life.

CHAPTER THREE

THE DISPENSING OF THE RICHES OF CHRIST BY THE SPIRIT

Scripture Reading: John 15:26; 16:13-15; 6:63a; 20:22; 1 Cor. 15:45b; 2 Cor. 3:6b, 17-18; Rom. 12:2-5; 1 Cor. 12:12-13

In the previous chapters we have seen that God's purpose is to have the church and that the church comes out of the dispensing of the riches of Christ. God's dispensing includes creation, incarnation, crucifixion, resurrection, ascension, descension, and eventually the rapture. Today we are still under the process of the dispensing of Christ. God's economy is to dispense Christ into us, and to dispense Christ into us simply means to work Christ into us. In the whole universe, what God has been doing and still is doing is to work Christ into us. This is what we call the economy of God, the dispensing of God.

The economy of God is simply a matter of the dispensing of Christ into all of us, and the issue of God's dispensing of Christ is the church. This kind of speaking is not common in today's Christianity. Perhaps many have never heard the term *the dispensing of Christ into us* or that God's economy is to work Christ into us. In Christianity we received many religious concepts. We heard that we were sinful and that we were going to hell, but God was so merciful to us that by His great love He loved us, He saved us, He granted us repentance, He gave us faith, He forgave all our sins, and He even regenerated us; now we are qualified to enter into the heavens to enjoy eternal life. Some have gone even further, saying that while we are on this earth we have to adjust ourselves, improve ourselves, and glorify the Father. I do not say that these concepts are wrong. They are not wrong, only too superficial, too shallow. They are too short of God's economy. Today in the Lord's recovery the Lord has shown us something deeper, something more solid. God's economy in this universe is not merely to save people from hell into heaven. God's economy is to have a corporate Body, a corporate man, which is the issue of the dispensing of all the riches of Christ. That is, God's economy is to work Christ into us.

We have been created by God. We do not care for Darwinism; we do not believe that we are the descendants of the apes. We are the creatures in God's creation, and God created us with a purpose. This purpose is that we would be a vessel. We are simply a vessel, a container. A vessel is made only to contain something. God in His creation made us containers, vessels, to contain Christ. This is fully revealed in Romans chapter nine. Romans 9 tells us that in God's creation we were made vessels unto honor, vessels of glory (vv. 21, 23), to contain a treasure, Christ. Second Corinthians 4:7 tells us that Christ is the treasure and we are the earthen vessels. Now the treasure is in the earthen vessels. It is not merely that we are convicted and forgiven of our sins. It is not simply that we are saved from hell and brought into heaven. The central point of God's intention, of God's economy, is that Christ has to be worked into us.

GOD'S INTENTION BEING RELATED TO HOW MUCH CHRIST WE HAVE

We are short of Christ. However, we may not have this concept. If a brother is wrong in his attitude to his wife, he may repent religiously, saying, "O Lord, I am wrong with my wife. Forgive me." By the Lord's mercy he may even go to his wife and say, "Please forgive me. I have been wrong in certain matters." This is good, but it is rather religious. If we have received a vision, a revelation, from God, we will not simply repent. We will realize that we are wrong because we are short of Christ. If we were not short of Christ, we would not be wrong, but if we are short of Christ, even to be right means nothing. Whether we are right or wrong makes no difference. Religiously it makes a difference, but spiritually it makes no difference. If a brother is short of Christ, whether he loses his temper with his wife or is good to her makes no difference. We may compare this brother to an electric lightbulb. If a lightbulb does not shine with electricity, it makes no difference if it is dirty or clean. We may wash the bulb, but it still does not have electricity. We are the vessels to contain Christ and to shine out Christ. Whether we are good or we are bad, whether we are a success or we are a failure, makes no difference as long as we are short of Christ. God does not care whether we are right or wrong. God cares for one thing—how much Christ we have.

To be right or wrong is according to the law, but today we are not in the dispensation of the law; we are in the dispensing of Christ. God has turned us from the law to Christ. God does not care merely whether we hate people or love people. This makes no difference. God cares for how much Christ we have. Praise the Lord, everyone among us has Christ, but the difference is in how much Christ we have. One may have much of Christ while another has only a little. God's intention, God's economy, is to work Christ into us. This is God's work. To adjust our temper does not mean anything. A wooden podium never loses its temper. In this sense it is much better than we are, but what good is this? God's intention is not a matter of not losing our temper. God's intention is related to how much Christ we have. It is not a matter of law. It is not a matter of what we do or do not do. It is a matter of how much Christ we have. Today we do not have the dispensation of good and evil; we have the dispensing of Christ. Therefore, we all need a turn.

We all need to have a renewed mind. In this country I have been speaking for nine years, and many have been listening to my messages for all these years. However, I still do not have much confidence that we all are clear about God's intention. Some may be clear in the meeting and may go home and say, "Hallelujah, now we are clear!" But the next morning they may be the same as they were nine years ago. If we lose our temper with our wife, we may know how to repent, but we may not realize that we are short of Christ. A sister who wears short skirts may receive the enlightenment that she is not proper. However, she should not merely repent concerning her clothes. She must realize that she wears such clothes because she is short of Christ. Similarly, a young brother should realize that he has long hair and a beard because he is short of Christ. Some who came among us with long hair eventually cut their hair. They did this because they had received more Christ. All our problems are due to our shortage of Christ. We must realize that we are short of Christ and that God's economy today is just to work Christ into us.

Many Christians today are divided. Christianity today has many divisions because Christians are short of Christ. If we are short of Christ today, tomorrow we may be divided. Division comes out of the shortage of Christ. For the proper church life we need an adequate measure of Christ. Without the proper measure of Christ we cannot have the proper church life because the church life is the issue of the dispensing of Christ, the issue of God's working of Christ into us. The proper church life is simply Christ Himself. How much church life we have depends on how much Christ we have. If we have more Christ, we have more church life. This is a very important matter. I look to the Lord for this. I do not care for a message, and I am not giving a lecture or a sermon. To speak eloquently does not mean anything. My burden is to stir us up and cause us to be troubled concerning our shortage of Christ. Christians today are too much at peace. We need this kind of trouble.

THE SPIRIT OF REALITY
FOR THE DISPENSING OF THE TRIUNE GOD

Sent by the Son from with the Father

The verses in the Scripture reading at the beginning of this chapter are firstly from the Gospel of John. The Gospel of John begins with "In the beginning was the Word, and the Word was with God, and the Word was God" (1:1). It goes on to say, "No one has ever seen God; the only begotten Son, who is in the bosom of the Father, He has declared Him" (v. 18). This book starts with God, goes on to show us the Father, and continues to show us that He is the Son. Hence we have God, the Father, and the Son. In 15:26 the Lord said, "But when the

Comforter comes, whom I will send to you from the Father, the Spirit of reality, who proceeds from the Father, He will testify concerning Me." In this verse the Son, not the Father, is the Sender of the Spirit. The Son sent the Spirit from the Father. *From* may be better translated as *from with* (see Darby's New Translation, 1:14, 15:26, and notes). The Spirit of reality comes not only from the Father but with the Father. When He comes, the Father comes. This verse reveals the reality of the Triune God. The Father, the Son, and the Spirit are here, and the Son is the Sender of the Spirit who comes from with the Father.

Making Christ Real to Us by His Dispensing

Moreover the Father, the Son, and the Spirit are one, but They are also three for dispensing. The Father is in the heavens, but the Son is here. Even though the Son was with the disciples, He could not enter into them. Therefore, there is the need of the Spirit. When the Spirit came, He entered into the disciples (14:17). This Spirit who is in us is the Spirit of reality. *The Spirit of reality* indicates that the Spirit makes everything the Son spoke to the disciples real. Jesus said, "I am the way and the reality and the life" (14:6). Without the Spirit entering into us, the Lord being life would not be real to us; it would merely be a doctrine. When the Spirit comes into us, He guides us into the reality that Christ is the life, because the Spirit is the reality of life. What Christ spoke was His word, but when the Spirit comes, He makes Christ's word real to us. The coming of the Spirit of reality is the dispensing of the Triune God, the dispensing of Christ into us.

As the Breath to Bring the Triune God into Us

We must read the Gospel of John again. First we have the Word and God. "In the beginning was the Word,...and the Word was God" (1:1). Then we have the Father, the Son, and the Spirit. Finally we have the breath (20:22). At the beginning of this book, in chapter one, is the Word which was God. At the end, in chapter twenty, is the breath. Do you believe that this breath is something separate from the Word? This breath is the Word, and this breath is also God, the Father, the

Son, and the Spirit. In this breath we have the Spirit, the Son, the Father, God, and the Word. This breath is the dispensing of Jesus, the dispensing of the Triune God into us. Today we receive the breath simply by breathing. By breathing this breath in, we receive the Spirit, the Son, the Father, God, and the Word. This is the dispensing of Jesus into us.

Becoming the Sevenfold Intensified Spirit for the Dispensing of God into Us

The Bible first reveals God, Jehovah, the Triune God. Genesis 1:1 says, "In the beginning God created the heavens and the earth." Following this, so many books in the Old Testament show us something about the Father. Then in the New Testament there are at least four books, the Gospels, about the Son. At the end of His life, the Son told us that He would send the Spirit from with the Father. From here we go on to the book of Acts. In the book of Acts we mainly have the Spirit. Then after all the Epistles is the last book, Revelation, which speaks of the sevenfold intensified Spirit (1:4; 4:5; 5:6). The Bible starts with God and ends with the sevenfold intensified Spirit. All this is for the dispensing of God into us.

Christ Becoming the Life-giving Spirit to Impart Life to Us

We may illustrate the dispensing of Christ with a watermelon. A watermelon is first cut into slices. Then the slices may be pressed into juice, which is so easy to drink. Melon, slices, and juice are the steps of the dispensing of the watermelon into us. God's intention is to dispense Himself into us, and the last step of His dispensing is the Spirit. John 6:63 says, "It is the Spirit who gives life." As the Spirit of reality He comes into us to bring us into all reality, but the main thing we must realize is that the Spirit imparts life into us. Who is this life-giving Spirit? John 6:63 must be connected to 1 Corinthians 15:45, which says, "The last Adam became a life-giving Spirit." It is the Spirit who gives life, and this life-giving Spirit is the last Adam, Jesus. Jesus, as the last Adam, was made a life-giving Spirit. Do not care for the distracting teachings of Christianity. Forget about those teachings and come back to the pure word. "The last Adam became a life-giving Spirit." "The Lord is the Spirit" (2 Cor. 3:17a), the Spirit who gives life. This is not my word; it is the pure word of the Bible.

In Darby's New Translation, 2 Corinthians 3:7 through 16 is parenthetical; verse 17 is a continuation of verse 6. In verses 6 and 17 Paul said, "Who has also made us sufficient as ministers of a new covenant, ministers not of the letter but of the Spirit; for the letter kills, but the Spirit gives life....And the Lord is the Spirit." God was God in Genesis, and He was the Father in the Old Testament. Then He became the Son in the four Gospels, and He became a life-giving Spirit in the Acts and in the Epistles. Then in the last book of the Bible, Revelation, He became the seven Spirits. Strictly speaking, today we are in the dispensing not of God the Father or even of the Son alone but of the Spirit. Today we are not even in Acts. I fully believe that today we are in the book of Revelation, the book of the sevenfold intensified Spirit. We must spend much time coming back to the Spirit because in the Lord's recovery nothing else is as important as this.

BEING FREED FROM THE BONDAGE OF THE LETTER

Second Corinthians 3:17 says, "And the Lord is the Spirit; and where the Spirit of the Lord is, there is freedom." According to the context of this chapter, *freedom* is the freedom from the bondage of the old teachings. In the ancient times many Christians were influenced by the teachings of Judaism. They were under a bondage, but Paul told them that they had the Spirit within them and were freed from the bondage of the Old Testament, the bondage of the letter of the Scriptures, the teachings of Judaism.

I am afraid that many Christians today are still under the bondage of the teachings of Christianity. We need a liberation. I was under this same bondage. It took me more than fifteen years to be liberated from all the old concepts I had received from the old teachings. Before I was liberated, I had many layers of veils, but where the Spirit of the Lord is, the veils are taken away. This is the real liberation. Many are still under the veils. They may pray-read the verses about which we are speaking, and they may attend the meetings, but they still may not be able to see. To be veiled is to be under a bondage. We need to be liberated, and to be liberated, according to 2 Corinthians 3, is to have all our veils removed.

BEING TRANSFORMED BY THE DISPENSING OF CHRIST

As we behold and reflect the Lord with an unveiled face, we are being transformed (v. 18). To be transformed is not to have an outward change. Outward change is not transformation. That is merely a kind of correction. Transformation is something from within. We may illustrate transformation by the color of a person's face. To color the face of a pale person is not transformation. This is only an outward correction. If, however, this person eats steak and chicken day by day, after a few months his face will be transformed from within. Transformation is a change in life, not merely a change in outward behavior according to the law or according to what is right. To be transformed into the image of the Lord is to be transformed from one degree of glory to another degree. Today a brother may be in one degree of glory, but after two weeks he may be in a second degree of glory, and after two months, he may be in yet another degree of glory.

Transformation is Christ dispensed into us. This is a change in life. When Christ is ministered and worked into us, we are transformed. This may be further illustrated by a glass of tea. Plain water can be transformed into tea by putting tea leaves into it. By putting tea into water, the water becomes "teaified." Originally, regardless of how pure and good we are, we are plain, like plain water. The more Christ as the "tea" is added into us, the more we are "Christified," that is, we are sanctified and transformed. To be transformed is just to have more Christ added into us.

TRANSFORMATION FOR THE BODY LIFE

Transformation is not merely for us to be sanctified, spiritual, or even marvelous and glorious. Concerning transformation, we have to go on from 2 Corinthians 3 to Romans 12: "And do not be fashioned according to this age, but be transformed by the renewing of the mind that you may prove what the will of God is, that which is good and well pleasing and perfect" (v. 2). Transformation is for the church life. It is for the Body. The will of God is the church, the Body life. This is confirmed by the verses following Romans 12:2. In verses 3 through 21 we see the Body. The will of God is not to prove what kind of marriage we should have, what kind of school we should attend, or what kind of house or car we should buy. It is that we get into the Body life. We must leave all these other things to the hand of God and simply be transformed by the renewing of our mind, that we may prove the will of God, that is, the Body life.

Christians today are mainly divided by opinions. Every Christian has his or her opinion. The way to be rid of all our opinions is by being transformed by the renewing of our mind. To be transformed is mainly to be renewed in our mind, and to be renewed in our mind is simply to be rid of all our opinions. Some dear ones may not care for our way of meeting. They may care to have a more quiet meeting. We may not like the noise in the meeting, but we have no choice. If we leave, we are divided and divisive. Therefore, we need to be renewed in our mind. If we are renewed in our minds by being rid of all our opinions, we will have the church life. If we are still bothered by the different things in Christian meetings, we are short of Christ.

Once when we were in New Zealand, I attended a small meeting in which there were more than twenty guitars. Nearly every young person brought a guitar to that meeting. If I had not had a proper measure of Christ, I might have walked out. That night, however, I not only had to stay but also to give a message. In my message I did not give them an unhappy face; rather, I gave them a smiling face. I was happy with all the guitars. Eventually I shortened my message and encouraged them to play more. It was a wonderful meeting. We need a proper measure of Christ. I do not care to see Christians dancing in a meeting, but sometimes some dear ones did dance. I was happy with them. Although I would not encourage dancing, by the measure of Christ I had no problem with them. This illustrates that we all need to be transformed.

In our early years in Los Angeles some brought tambourines to the meetings. Some of the brothers were angry with this. I asked one such brother, "In the eyes of the Lord, what is the difference between a tambourine and a piano?" He admitted that there was no difference in the eyes of God, but that there was a great difference in his eyes. I did not speak a word to rebuke him, but I fully realized that in this dear saint there was a shortage of Christ. After a couple of days I went to see the ones who played the tambourines. They also were short of Christ. They said that without the tambourines they could not release their spirit. If we need a tambourine to help us to release the spirit, we are short of the Spirit, short of Christ. There is no use in arguing with people who are short of Christ. Do not rebuke them. They are simply short of Christ. We all must see that we need a proper measure of Christ. We need Christ to be worked into us more and more.

The church life is the issue of the dispensing of Christ. The church life is the Body, and the Body is Christ. First Corinthians 12:12 says, "For even as the body is one and has many members, yet all the members of the body, being many, are one body, so also is the Christ." In ourselves we are not one Body, but in the Spirit we are one Body. Verse 13 says, "For also in one Spirit we were all baptized into one body, whether Jews or Greeks, whether slaves or free, and were all given to drink one Spirit." To be in the spirit is to terminate our nature and to have all that Christ is to us. It is to terminate what we are and to take what Christ is. This is the church life and this is the Body. Today, especially in America, there is the wrong concept that we can have the Body life by teaching. We can never have a proper Body life by teaching. Neither can we have a proper Body life by the gifts. It is possible to have the Body only by Christ as life, so we all have to take Christ as our life. To take Christ as life is the dispensing of Christ for the church, the Body. The Body life which we have is simply Christ as the Spirit.

CHAPTER FOUR

THE DISPENSING OF THE RICHES OF CHRIST
THROUGH HIS WORD

Scripture Reading: John 1:1, 14; 4:24; 5:39-40; 6:35a, 57b, 63;
14:23; 15:7-8; 17:17; 1 John 5:6b; Col. 3:16; Eph. 5:18-19;
6:17-18; Jer. 15:16

In the previous chapters we saw that the eternal purpose
of God is to have the church, that the church comes out of the
dispensing of the riches of Christ, and that in His economy
God eventually became the all-inclusive Spirit. It is by this
Spirit that all the riches of Christ are being dispensed into us.

THE WORD OF GOD BEING GOD HIMSELF

In this chapter we come to the Word of God. We all know
that the Bible is the word of God. However, we probably know
this in a very common, natural, or religious way. We see that
the word in the Scriptures is the Word of God, but we need to
see something more. John 1:1 says, "In the beginning was the
Word, and the Word was with God, and the Word was God."
The Word is not only the word of God; the Word is God Himself. In the beginning was the Word, this Word was God, and
one day this Word became flesh, tabernacling among us, full
of grace and reality (v. 14). *Grace* means enjoyment. The Word,
who was God becoming flesh and tabernacling among us, was
full not of doctrines and teachings but of enjoyment and reality. To be sure, this Word is more than the word of God in
letters. This Word is God Himself.

THE WORD OF GOD BEING THE EMBODIMENT OF GOD

The word in the Bible is not only the word of God; it is also
the embodiment of God. When we touch the word, we must

touch God Himself. It is short and even wrong to touch the word in the Bible and not touch God Himself. The Lord Jesus told the Jewish leaders, "You search the Scriptures, because you think that in them you have eternal life; and it is these that testify concerning Me. Yet you are not willing to come to Me that you may have life" (5:39-40). The word *search* in Greek means to research, to search and search again. The Lord Jesus seemed to say, "I am one with the Scriptures, and the Scriptures are one with Me. If you come to the Scriptures, you have to come to Me. If you research the Scriptures, you have to come to Me. You have to make the Scriptures one with Me; instead, you have made the Scriptures something separate from Me. Therefore, you are wrong. You may gain knowledge in letters from the Scriptures, but you cannot have life because I am life."

These two verses are a warning to us. It is possible to come to the Bible yet not come to the Lord. It is possible to separate the Bible from the Lord. We have to realize that to divorce the Bible from Christ is seriously wrong. All the time we have to take the Bible as one with the Lord. Whenever we come to the Bible, we have to come to the Lord. Whenever we read the Bible, we have to touch the Lord. The Bible is not merely a book of knowledge. The Bible is the embodiment of the Lord Himself.

THE BIBLE BEING THE MEANS OF GOD'S DISPENSING

God's intention in His economy is to dispense Christ into us, and for this dispensing there must be some means. The Bible is the means that God uses to dispense Christ into us. To be sure, if we come to touch the means without touching Christ, we are wrong. In order to serve a meal we must have some utensils, such as bowls, dishes, and cups, but if we come to the bowls, dishes, and cups and do not touch any food, we are very foolish. We do not come to dinner for the bowls, dishes, or cups; we come to dinner for the food. Still, in order to serve the food we must have the means. The Bible is the means through which God dispenses Christ into us. Therefore, when we come to touch the Bible, our intention is not merely to touch the Bible. The Bible is only the means; Christ

Himself is the food. If we come to the Bible without coming to Jesus, we are wrong.

LEARNING TO TOUCH THE SPIRIT
AND LIFE IN THE BIBLE

There is a further problem, which is related to our different organs. As humans we have eyes and ears, and we have something deeper, which is our mind and heart. In addition, we have something even deeper, which is our human spirit. In John 4:24 the Lord Jesus gave us a principle. He said, "God is Spirit, and those who worship Him must worship in spirit and truthfulness." God is Spirit, so in order to worship Him, we have to worship Him in our spirit. The principle is that the way to worship Spirit is with our spirit. It is only possible for spirit to worship Spirit. In the same way, we must realize that the words in the Bible are not mere letters. Apparently, all the words in the Bible are letters printed on paper, but in actuality they are spirit and life (John 6:63). Since the words of the Bible are spirit, we have to exercise our spirit to touch the Word. Only our spirit can touch the Spirit.

We may illustrate this in the following way. Outwardly, a man appears to have only a physical body, but inwardly, he has a mind to consider and understand things and a heart to love and seek things. He also has a spirit to contact, receive, and contain God. If I shake hands with him, I make outward contact with his physical body. If while I am shaking hands, he looks at me and I look at him, there is also a communication between our two minds. If I smile at him and he responds by smiling back at me, then a deeper communication, a communication between the hearts, takes place. Then if I say, "Praise the Lord!", and he responds by saying, "Amen!", we have communicated in the spirit.

The Bible also has a "body." The body of the Bible is the black and white letters. The first part of John 3:16 says, "For God so loved the world." The letters that spell these words are the body of this verse. However, in the body of the Bible there is spirit and life. When we exercise our mind to read the letters of the Bible, we touch only the body of the Bible, but when we exercise our spirit, we touch spirit and life.

The Bible is the means for God's dispensing. God's dispensing is to dispense Christ into us, and the Bible is the means used by God to do this. Christ as the all-inclusive Spirit is abstract and mysterious, but in the Bible He becomes solid. We can touch the Bible, hold it, and carry it anywhere, but we still must open it, open our spirit, and open our mouth to utter something from the Bible to the Lord. In this way we receive the Spirit and life.

THE OUTWARD WAY AND THE INWARD WAY
TO TOUCH THE BIBLE

There are two ways to touch the Bible: the outward way and the inward way. The outward way to touch the Bible is by exercising our mind merely to understand it, while the inward way is by using our spirit not mainly to understand it but to touch the spirit and get the life supply.

John 1:1 is a wonderful verse. Suppose two brothers come together to read this verse. After reading it, one brother may ask, "What does *in the beginning* mean?" The other brother may say, "God is the beginning." The first brother may respond, "I don't think so. How can you say that God is the beginning? I don't understand what you are talking about. And what is *the Word*? This verse says that the Word was with God and the Word was God. Surely the Word and God are two. How can they be one? Let us ask the students at the Bible institute." This is an illustration of touching the Bible in an outward way. Touching the Bible even for only a few minutes in this way is deadening.

There is another way to touch the Bible, the inward way, the way of exercising our spirit. Suppose these same two brothers come to the Word in the following way, saying, "O Lord, in the beginning. In the beginning was the Word. Amen! Hallelujah for the beginning. O Lord, the Word. Hallelujah, for the Word! And the Word was with God. O God! And the Word was God!" When we exercise our spirit to touch the Word in such a living way, we may not understand much, but we are filled with the Spirit, and we get the life supply.

It is very clear that the Bible can be two entities. It can be dead letters to kill us, or it can be the Spirit to enliven us. It depends upon which way we touch it. If we touch the Bible in an outward way using only our mind, we will be deadened. However, if we touch the Bible in an inward way exercising our spirit, we will be enlivened. This is true of any verse or chapter, from the first verse of Genesis to the last verse of Revelation. Sometimes we may not understand what we read, and sometimes we may understand but not be able to utter what we see. We may even say, "Praise the Lord, I received something this morning, but I do not have the words to speak it!" This is the right way. The right way to touch the Bible is to touch the Lord Himself. We must never separate the Bible from the Lord. Whenever we open the Bible, we have to open our mouth and open our spirit to utter something to the Lord. We can say, "O Lord! O Lord Jesus!" The louder we say these words the better. This is truly something wonderful and marvelous.

Today the best dietitians cannot fully tell us what is in the food that we eat day by day. If the smallest wheat germ cannot be fully understood, how can we understand the Bible in full? Although we do not fully understand the food we eat, we still take it in day by day. Many things get into us and nourish us, whether or not we understand them. It is the same with the Bible. The Bible is not merely for our understanding. If the Bible were only for our understanding, we would be miserable because our understanding is so limited. We should not trust in our understanding of the Bible. Forty years ago I trusted very much in my understanding of the Bible, but today I no longer trust in my understanding. I do not care merely to understand the Bible. When I come to the Bible, I simply receive it. I receive it not merely by using my mind to understand but by exercising my spirit. I may say, "O Lord! Amen. In the beginning. Hallelujah, for the beginning! Oh, hallelujah, for the beginning! In the beginning was the Word. I don't know what the Word is, and I don't know what the beginning is, but I do know that in the beginning was the Word!" This is a marvelous way to touch the Bible. In this way we get the Spirit and life from the Bible.

Many Christians appreciate that the Bible is a wonderful book. Yet the Bible is more than a wonderful book; it is the

embodiment of Christ. The way we touch the Bible deter-
mines whether or not we touch Christ. If we touch the Bible
only by using our mind, we are finished. To touch the Bible in
this way makes us like the Jews who researched the Bible
without touching the Lord Jesus. This is the wrong way.
Whenever we pick up the Bible with our hand, immediately
we have to stir up our spirit. Whenever we open the Bible, we
have to open our mouth, and whenever we read a word in the
Bible, we have to utter it from our spirit.

PRACTICING TO PRAY-READ THE WORD OF GOD

Our coming to the Bible should always be our coming to
the Lord Jesus. The Bible should always be one with the Lord.
If we do not understand the Bible, we should not be bothered.
This does not mean very much. If we do not understand, we
may let it go for the present time. We should not be occupied
with trying to understand the Bible. We should simply receive
it.

When we open to John 1:1, we should not merely read it.
We have to utter it by exercising our spirit. We can say, "In the
beginning! O Lord, in the beginning. Hallelujah, in the beginning!" To utter something by exercising our spirit makes
reading the Bible very different. If someone has never tasted
pray-reading, I would beg him to try it. Once you taste it, you
will never drop it. You will become "addicted" to pray-reading
the Word of God. If you are afraid of losing your face, you can
go into your room, close the door, and try it a little bit. Change
your way of touching the Bible. Formerly, you may have
always touched the Bible by reading it and exercising your
mind, but now you must change from this way to exercising
your spirit. Before you read, you can loudly say, "O Lord
Jesus!" But if you are afraid of losing your face, you can call on
the Lord and pray-read softly. I believe that if you try this for
ten minutes, you will taste something. You will realize the difference between your former way and this way. You will touch
the living Lord, and then you will come to the meeting, jump
up, and say, "Hallelujah! Now I know! The words of the Bible
are the Spirit! There are many verses that I don't understand,
but I touch the Spirit."

If we open up the book of Daniel, where there are many puzzling verses, we can still touch the Spirit. Daniel 9:24-27 speaks of seventy weeks, which are divided into seven weeks, sixty-two weeks, and one week. These seventy weeks are very puzzling. However, if we go to this book and say, "O Lord, the seventy weeks. Hallelujah for the first week. I don't know what a 'week' is, but I do know that there is a week. Amen! Praise the Lord for the seven weeks, amen for the sixty-two weeks, and hallelujah for the last week!" In our mind we may not get much, but in our spirit, we will be filled with the Lord as the Spirit (2 Cor. 3:17). This is marvelous! Eventually, we cannot say that we did not get anything in our mind. At the very least, we know that there are seven weeks, sixty-two weeks, and the last week.

Try coming to the Bible in this way. One day the light will come, and we will have the living understanding. At that time, it will not be something taught by others; it will be something enlightened by the Spirit. While we are pray-reading, we may think that we do not understand anything, but later, perhaps the next day, or after two weeks, two months, or even a year, the light will spring up from within us, and we will say, "Now I understand the seventy weeks of Daniel 9." At such a time our understanding will be something living.

PRAY-READING TO RECEIVE
THE DISPENSING OF THE RICHES OF CHRIST

At any time—day or night, morning or evening—we can open up the Bible and pray-read a few verses. When we do, we receive the Spirit. In other words, we receive the riches of Christ. The riches of Christ are unsearchable, unlimited, and unspeakable. No one can tell out all the riches of Christ. Christ is in every chapter and every verse because the Spirit of Christ is in the word.

When we come to pray-read Genesis 1:1, Christ may not seem to be there according to the letter. As we read, "In the beginning God created the heavens and the earth," we may find no direct mention of Christ. However, if we exercise our spirit to pray-read this verse, after a few minutes we will receive something of Christ within. Christ will become so precious within us. Nothing of Christ is mentioned in this verse, yet after pray-reading it, we have the sweet sense and the sweet taste of Christ. It is wonderful that there is something of Christ in every verse and in every word of the Bible.

If we would pray-read chapter by chapter and book by book, week after week, month after month, and year after year, gradually we will receive enlightenment, and all the things of Christ will spring up within us. All the riches of Christ will become our enjoyment. At this time it may be that there is no need for us to open up the Bible because so much of it is within us. Throughout the day, these things within us become our enjoyment of Christ. In this way all the riches of Christ are ministered and dispensed into us. This dispensing will transform us and cause us to have a metabolic change, a change in life. This change comes about because so many heavenly elements of Christ are added into us. These heavenly elements and spiritual ingredients will cause us to have not only an outward change but a metabolic change, a change in life. All these new elements will replace and discharge all the old things. This is a metabolic change, transforming us into a new condition.

A certain brother may have been saved two months ago, and now he is in the church life. However, he may not have much element of the truth within him. He does not have a supply for the church life because the riches of Christ have been dispensed into him only for a short time. He should not be disappointed. Rather, he simply needs to pray-read more. He needs to pray-read day by day, verse after verse, chapter after chapter, and book after book. It is best if he would pray-read ten times a day; this is not too much. If he pray-reads for three months in this way, there will be a metabolic change within him, and he will have the element of Christ within him for the church life. After a time, the church will be enriched by what he is, because the church life is the issue of the enjoyment of Christ, which comes from the dispensing of the riches of Christ.

Paul speaks of pray-reading in Ephesians 6:17-18a, which says, "And receive the helmet of salvation and the sword of the Spirit, which Spirit is the word of God, by means of all prayer and petition, praying at every time in spirit." To take the word not by reading only but by means of all prayer is to pray-read. Andrew Murray also said that we must read the word prayerfully. To read the Bible prayerfully is to pray-read. Even from our own experiences we can testify that we pray-read the Word of God without realizing it. We may have read a verse and immediately turned it into a prayer. That was pray-reading. Many of us have done this in the past.

PRAY-READING TO ENJOY CHRIST

The Lord has shown us in a definite way that we must practice pray-reading. In my Christian experience no other way can replace pray-reading. The best way to have the enjoyment of Christ is to pray-read. We all have to try it and see.

The Bible is the embodiment of Christ. All the riches of Christ are embodied in the Bible. The Bible has many pages, and each page contains the riches of Christ. Therefore, day by day, we have to pray-read. Eventually, through our pray-reading we will see that Christ is God, the Lamb, the Creator, the creature, the Father, the Son, the Spirit, life, light, love, the King, the Priest, the Prophet, every kind of tree, wheat, corn, milk, honey, water, green grass, tender pasture, and the cattle. We will discover that Christ is every positive thing in the universe. This Christ is also the building, the house, the bedroom, the living room, the kitchen, the window, and the door. We will also find that Christ is the good land, the sun, and the morning star.

After pray-reading for half a year, we will be disgusted with every kind of religious service. We may say, "I don't need to listen to a sermon or a message. I have something better. I have something richer. I have something sweeter." All the riches of Christ are in the Bible. However, we cannot merely meditate over it. Meditation is too poor. Rather, we should open the Word and eat it by pray-reading. We may say, "O Lord, Your words were found and I ate them" (Jer. 15:16). In this way we take in the riches of Christ. The riches of Christ are in every verse.

DIGESTING THE WORD OF GOD
FOR THE INCREASE OF THE MEASURE OF CHRIST

Good digestion is always needed with eating. In our physical body, good digestion gives the food a free way throughout the body. The best digestion occurs when the food that gets into our stomach has a free course to get into our whole system. This affords us the best nourishment. On the other hand, we have indigestion when due to some blockage our food does not have a free course in us.

I must warn you. Pray-reading is wonderful, but we also have to pray, "Lord, clear a way within me. O Lord, have a free course within me." Pray-reading does not help us to obtain mere knowledge; rather, it brings many things of the Lord into us. Therefore, we need to give the things of the Lord a free course within us. This affords us the best spiritual digestion, assimilating what we have pray-read. Never say no to the Lord; learn always to say amen.

Whether or not we understand what we pray-read, it always brings something of the Lord into us. When these things get into us, they need a free course. Thus, we always have to say amen. The Lord, the Word, and the Spirit are one. The Lord is the Word, the Word is the Spirit, and the Spirit is the Lord. When we get the Word into us, we have the Spirit and we have the Lord. Therefore, we must be warned. If we pray-read for ten minutes, we may not understand much, but we will sense that something is within us. We may say that it is the Word, we may say that it is the Spirit, or we may say that it is the Lord. Whatever term we use, there will be something moving within us and adjusting us.

After pray-reading, we may have the intention to go fishing, but something within us indicates that we should not go. Is it the Word, is it the Spirit, or is it the Lord? It is hard to say. It is not even a "gentle, quiet voice" (1 Kings 19:12). In Christianity many like to talk about the gentle, quiet voice, but that is something of the Old Testament. What is within us is not a voice or a clear word such as "don't" or "do." There is simply a sensation within us, indicating that we should not go. What should we do at that time? We have to say, "Amen, Lord. Amen." However, nine out of ten times we may still go.

This blocks the course within us. Then after two or three times like this, we may realize that our pray-reading does not work very well, and we may even lose our appetite for pray-reading. The reason for this is indigestion. When we try to pray-read, it does not taste as sweet. However, if we will say, "Amen, Lord," every time something within us forbids us, restricts us, adjusts us, or corrects us, we will be hungry for pray-reading.

Sometimes when I am at home, I suddenly say, "Amen." My family may check with me and ask, "What happened? To whom are you saying amen?" In response to them I say, "You don't know, but I know." I am saying amen to the word of the Spirit, the Lord within me who is moving, speaking, anointing, and adjusting. If we would say amen in this way once, twice, or even three times, we will be hungry for pray-reading. Then pray-reading will taste so good. We will have a good appetite because we have had the best digestion. Later, others will see a change of life in us. No one has taught us, rebuked us, corrected us, or instructed us, yet there is a change. Even as we are changing, we do not realize the change. Something subconsciously and unconsciously is changing us. This is the growth in life, and this is the increase of the measure of Christ. This proves that some of the riches of Christ have been dispensed into us.

Reading a message like this may help us, but the best way to pick up the riches of Christ is pray-reading. By pray-reading two birds are killed with one stone. When we pray-read, we pray and at the same time we read. This is why it is called *pray-reading*. This kind of prayer is not a peculiar prayer or a prayer with vain words. It is prayer using the wonderful Word. In this way we get into all the riches of Christ. This is what we need in our Christian life. Pick up pray-reading and try it. It will turn us around a hundred and eighty degrees. If we would pick up pray-reading in a proper way, we will be another kind of Christian after only one week. We will see the Lord's recovery, we will see God's will, and we will see the church. Then we will see that Christ is so different to us. This is the means that God uses to dispense Christ into us.

CHAPTER FIVE

GOD IN CHRIST AS OUR FOOD

Scripture Reading: Col. 1:15a; 3:4a; John 6:57; 1 Cor. 8:1; Rev. 2:7b, 17; 22:2a, 14

From the beginning God has had an intention, but this intention was neglected by the entire human race. When the Lord Jesus came, He labored to restore God's intention and to bring people back to the beginning. Eventually, the church was produced in order to pay its full attention to the original intention of God. Shortly after the church was established, however, the church also neglected God's intention.

THE LORD'S PROMISE TO THE OVERCOMERS CONCERNING EATING

After the degradation of the church, the Lord sounded a call for overcomers in the book of Revelation (2:7, 11, 17, 26; 3:5, 12, 21). He promised to give these overcomers to eat according to His original intention, that is, to eat of the tree of life (2:7), to eat of the hidden manna (v. 17), and to dine, to feast, with Him (3:20). The Lord's promise to the overcomers reminds us of three significant times of eating in the Old Testament: 1) the eating of the tree of life in the garden of Eden as a sign to the man created by God; 2) the eating of manna as a blessing to God's people while they wandered in the wilderness; and 3) the eating of the produce of the good land in the yearly feasts.

To eat of the tree of life is to eat according to God's original intention in the garden of Eden, to eat the manna is to enjoy the daily food of God's people in the wilderness, and to feast with the Lord is to enjoy the rich produce in the good land. When the children of Israel entered into the good land, they began to enjoy the rich produce from the good land (Josh. 5:12). Then they were commanded by God to hold three feasts a year: the feast of the Passover (the Feast of Unleavened Bread), Pentecost (the Feast of Weeks), and the Feast of Tabernacles (Deut. 16:16). The Lord's promise in the book of Revelation brings us back to God's original intention in the beginning.

GOD'S INTENTION IN THE BIBLE

God's intention in the Bible is very basic, but it has been hidden for centuries. Genesis 1 tells us that God created man in His own image and gave him dominion over all the created things (v. 26). Two words here are very important: *image* and *dominion*. God created man in His own image, and God gave man dominion over all things, especially over the earth and the creeping things. The Bible then tells us that God put this man in front of the tree of life (2:9). Many trees were in the garden, and all were good for food, but only one tree was designated with the name *the tree of life*.

Colossians 1:15 tells us wonderfully that Jesus is the image of God. This verse brings us back to Genesis 1 where man was made in the image of God. Who is the image of God, and what is the image of God? According to Colossians 1:15, Christ is the image of God. Man was created in God's image, and God's image is Christ. Man, therefore, was made according to Christ. This is wonderful! We must be deeply impressed with the two words *image* and *dominion*. God made man in His own image and gave man dominion over all the earth.

In Genesis 2 God formed Adam's physical body with the dust of the ground (v. 7a). According to medical doctors, man's physical body contains all the elements of the dust, including salt, copper, iron, sulfur, and many other items. This proves that man is simply dust. Then after creating man's body, God breathed into his nostrils the breath of life (v. 7b). According to the Hebrew text, the word *breath* in Genesis 2:7 is the same word translated *spirit* in Proverbs 20:27, which says, "The spirit of man is the lamp of Jehovah." God breathed the breath of life into man's body of dust, and this breath is the spirit of man. After God breathed into man's body, forming his spirit, man became a living soul.

THE TREE OF LIFE BEING GOD IN CHRIST
AS LIFE IN THE FORM OF FOOD

Having the image of God and the authority of God are mainly objective. Subjectively, man still needed the life of God. Man had the image of God, and he also had the dominion of God, but he still did not have the life of God, which is God Himself. Therefore, God put man in front of the tree of life in the midst of the garden (Gen. 2:8-9), indicating by this that man should partake of it. The tree of life signifies God Himself as life to man in the form of food. Later, the Bible indicates to us that God in Christ is the tree of life (John 1:4; 10:10; 14:6; 15:1). Genesis 2:9 says, "And out of the ground Jehovah God caused to grow every tree that is pleasant to the sight and good for food, as well as the tree of life in the middle of the garden." Then when Jesus came, He said, "I am the bread of life; he who comes to Me shall by no means hunger, and he who believes into Me shall by no means ever thirst....I am the living bread which came down out of heaven; if anyone eats of this bread, he shall live forever....As the living Father has sent Me and I live because of the Father, so he who eats Me, he also shall live because of Me" (John 6:35, 51, 57).

GOD'S COMMANDMENT
CONCERNING MAN'S EATING

According to Genesis 2:9, the tree of knowledge was next to the tree of life. God put man in front of the tree of life so that he would take the tree of life, and He also warned man not to take of the tree of knowledge. Genesis 2:16-17 says, "And Jehovah God commanded the man, saying, Of every tree of the garden you may eat freely, but of the tree of the knowledge of good and evil, of it you shall not eat; for in the day that you eat of it you shall surely die." The tree of knowledge is the tree of the knowledge not only of evil but of good and evil. Both good and evil are versus life. God's intention was that Adam would take the tree of life and have nothing to do with the tree of the knowledge of good and evil.

After man's creation, God gave Adam almost no commandments. He did not say, "Adam, first, you have to realize that
you must worship Me. I am the Creator and you are the creature. Second, you have to glorify Me. Third, I made a wife for
you, and you have to love her. Fourth, you have to be kind,
humble, and patient. Last, I will give you some children, and
you have to take care of them." Such commandments are not
found in Genesis 2. God told man very little of what to do and
what not to do. God only told him to be careful about the tree
of the knowledge of good and evil. In other words, God seemed
to say, "Adam, just take care of your eating. If you eat the right
things, you will be okay, but if you eat the wrong things, you
will die." God did not tell Adam to do anything. He did not
give him ten commandments nor even two commandments.
He simply warned Adam to eat rightly, to be careful concerning the two trees which were in front of him. We all must
realize that God's intention is not that we do this or that.
God's intention is that we eat of Him and take Him as our life.

TAKING GOD AS LIFE BY EATING JESUS

God's intention was that He would be Adam's life, that is,
that Adam would take God as his life. We may illustrate the
way to take God as life with American produce. How can a
chicken become life to us? If we only carry the chicken around,
it is still a whole chicken; it is not life to us. The only way for
the chicken to be life to us is for us to slaughter it, cook it,
serve it on the dining table, and eat it. Then after a few hours
of digestion and assimilation, the chicken will become us. It is
only in this way that something outside of us can become life
to us. We have the saying, "You are what you eat." I may see a
chicken at your home in the morning, but in the evening it
may be gone. Where is the chicken? It is now in you; after
eating the chicken, you become the chicken.

Few if any in Christianity have heard that God's intention
is that man would take God by eating Him. Many have never
heard a message that told them that man has to eat God.
During a conference in Taiwan in 1958 I gave a strong
message on John 6, telling the saints that Jesus is eatable and
that we all have to eat Him. After the meeting, an educated

brother came to me in a very nice but purposeful way, saying, "Brother Lee, your message tonight was wonderful. Only one thing bothered me. You said that we can eat Jesus. To say this is too wild." I replied, "Brother, if I am wild, I am not the first one to be wild. The Lord Jesus Himself was wild because He said in John 6:57, 'He who eats Me, he also shall live because of Me.' This is not my invention; this is my quotation. Don't blame me for being wild. Go to the Lord Jesus and blame Him."

Actually, it is not a matter of being wild. Thoughts like these come from the human and religious concepts. Whenever we talk about God, we always consider that God is so great, so high, and so dignified, sitting on the throne, and that we have to bow down before Him. This is our natural, religious concept. When someone says that we can eat Jesus, we wonder how Jesus can be eaten. In John 6 the Lord Jesus performed a miracle by feeding five thousand people with five barley loaves. The Jewish people saw that miracle and, considering that Jesus was someone great, wanted to make Him a king. Eventually, the Lord Jesus withdrew from them because He did not want to be their king outwardly. The next day when He came back, He told the people, "I am the bread of life. I have no intention to be something great. My intention is to be your food. Don't make Me a king. Rather, take Me as food and eat Me."

To kneel down quietly before the Lord as the bread on the table is too religious. The Lord Jesus may say, "Silly ones. I don't want to see you bowing down. Get up and eat. I don't want your religious worship. It is not that I am short of your worship; it is that you are short of Me. You have to take Me in by eating Me."

REMEMBERING THE LORD
BY EATING AND DRINKING HIM

Many of us have been taught that in the Lord's table meeting we should remember the Lord by exercising our mind to recall how the Lord was the One on the throne in the heavens, how one day He became a little child born in a manger, how He lived in a carpenter's home, how He came out to carry out His ministry, how He was persecuted, arrested, tested, sentenced, and brought to Calvary, and how He was put on the cross. I had this kind of remembrance many times when I was young.

However, in Matthew 26:26 the Lord said, "Take, eat; this is My body," and in Luke 22:19 He said, "This is My body which is being given for you; do this in remembrance of Me." In the same way He spoke of the cup, saying, "This cup is the new covenant established in My blood; this do, as often as you drink it, unto the remembrance of Me" (1 Cor. 11:25). What is the way to remember the Lord? The proper remembrance of the Lord is not to recall Him but to take Him in. God's concept is that we must eat Him.

GOD IN CHRIST AS OUR FOOD
REVEALED IN THE OLD TESTAMENT

The Passover Lamb

God in Christ to be our life in the form of food is revealed, typified, and prefigured in many ways in the Old Testament. For instance, at the time of the Passover there was not only the sprinkled blood; there was also the meat of the lamb for the people to eat with the unleavened bread (Exo. 12:3-11). Many in Christianity pay their full attention to the sprinkling of the blood, but they neglect the eating of the lamb. We must realize that the sprinkling of the blood is for the eating of the lamb. The sprinkling of the blood upon the doorposts of the children of Israel was a covering, but at the time that they were to leave Egypt, they needed food to sustain them. Under the covering of the blood they could eat the meat of the lamb so that they would be prepared to walk out of Egypt.

The lamb of the Passover was a type of Christ (1 Cor. 5:7). Today Jesus is our Passover Lamb. His blood was sprinkled for us (1 Pet. 1:2), and He Himself is good for food. When we believe into the Lord Jesus, we eat Him under the covering of His blood. Today Christianity preaches the sprinkling of the blood yet neglects the matter of eating Jesus. Under the sprinkling of the blood we need the eating of Jesus. Christians who have been saved for many years may never have realized that their need is to eat Jesus. We all need to eat Jesus.

Manna

After the people came out of Egypt, they entered into the wilderness and wandered for forty years. Day by day they ate manna (Exo. 16:35). Many Christians know that manna is a type of Christ, but when I was in Christianity I never heard anyone say that we have to eat Jesus day by day. Some did say that we have to take the word from the Bible as our daily portion. This is not bad, but it is not good enough. We need to realize that manna is a type not only of the word as our daily portion; manna is Jesus Himself. Jesus is our daily food, our daily portion.

The Good Land

After the people entered into the good land and they ate of the rich produce of the land, the manna ceased (Josh. 5:12). The good land is Christ (Col. 1:12; Eph. 3:8). I hope that you all will read *The All-inclusive Christ,* published by Living Stream Ministry. It helps us to see that Christ today is the rich land, flowing with milk and honey. He is so rich, but we must labor on Him.

Manna is wonderful, but manna has an aspect which is not so good: God never asked His people to worship Him with manna. Manna was good but it could not constitute a proper worship to God. However, God did ask His people to worship Him with all the rich produce of the good land (Deut. 12:11). They had to bring all the offerings—the cattle, the firstborn ones, and the top produce of the good land—to God as their worship.

By the foregoing word we can realize that beginning from Genesis 1 there is always the concept of eating: eating the tree of life, eating the manna, and eating the rich produce of the good land.

CHRIST BEING THE CHILDREN'S BREAD
AND THE CRUMBS UNDER THE TABLE

We can do nothing without eating. Today we simply need to eat Christ. He is our life in the form of food. Christ came to present Himself as the bread of life. One day a Canaanite woman came to Him, saying, "Have mercy on me, Lord, Son of David!" The Lord Jesus answered, "It is not good to take the children's bread and throw it to the little dogs" (Matt. 15:22, 26). This was quite meaningful. The woman called the Lord Jesus the Son of David, a descendant of the royal family, but the Lord Jesus in His answer indicated that He was bread for the children. The Lord seemed to say, "Don't consider that I am the royal descendant. I have come here as bread to you. I am the bread to the children. Consider Me in this way." The woman was clever and immediately took her position. She said, "Yes, Lord. You are right. You are the bread to the children, and I am a Gentile dog. Yet even the dogs have their portion—the crumbs under the table. You, Jesus, are now under the table. You have been thrown off the table by the naughty Jewish people. Now it is my turn. You are on the Gentile floor as crumbs to be my portion." The natural, human, and religious concepts are that Jesus is the Son of David, of the royal family, even the King. The divine concept, however, is that Jesus as the very God has come to be our life in the form of food. Therefore, we must eat Him.

KNOWLEDGE AND GIFTS DISTRACTING THE BELIEVERS FROM CHRIST AS THEIR LIFE

Jesus died on the cross, and in resurrection He was transfigured from the flesh into the Spirit, as 1 Corinthians 15:45b says, "The last Adam became a life-giving Spirit." In the book of 1 Corinthians Paul points out that the Corinthian believers' need was not gifts or knowledge but the life-giving Spirit and the eating of Jesus. The Corinthian believers made the mistake of taking knowledge and gifts. First Corinthians 1:7 says, "So that you do not lack in any gift, eagerly awaiting the revelation of our Lord Jesus Christ." The Corinthians did not lack in any gift. They had all the gifts, and they had all knowledge, but they were not matured saints. Chapter three says, "And I, brothers, was not able to speak to you as to spiritual men, but as to fleshy, as to infants in Christ" (v. 1). The Corinthians had knowledge, but they were still infants.

In 8:1 Paul said, "Knowledge puffs up." Knowledge kills us because knowledge is something of the tree of knowledge. It is not something of the tree of life. The Corinthians held the concept that they needed knowledge and gifts, but according to Paul they were still infants. The apostle Paul's concept was that they needed to eat Christ. In 10:3 and 4 Paul says, "And all ate the same spiritual food, and all drank the same spiritual drink; for they drank of a spiritual rock which followed them, and the rock was Christ." In chapter three Paul said, "I gave you milk to drink" (v. 2). The Corinthians wrongly took knowledge and the gifts, so Paul adjusted them by telling them that their need was Christ as their food. The last Adam became the Spirit who gives life. They needed to take in this Christ. The church has missed the mark, not only today in this century but even in the first century. The Corinthians missed the mark by turning aside from the eating of Jesus to knowledge and gifts. As a result, the church became degraded. The degradation of the church came from emphasizing teachings, knowledge, and gifts.

BEING RECOVERED FROM TEACHINGS AND DOCTRINES TO THE EATING OF JESUS

In the seven epistles in Revelation, the Lord Jesus spoke to the churches concerning teachings and works (2:2, 6, 14-15, 20). He seemed to be saying, "You have the teaching of Balaam, you have the teaching of the Nicolaitans, and you are taught by the woman Jezebel. You also have done many things for Me. You have knowledge, you have the doctrines, you have teachings, and you have all the gifts. However, you have missed eating Me." In these seven epistles, the Lord Jesus promised the overcomers that they would eat. He did not promise them to know, to do, or to work, but to eat of the tree of life. This is the Lord's recovery. Are you recovered? Today many of us talk much about the recovery, but I must check with you: What is the Lord's recovery? The recovery is to bring us back to the origin, back to the beginning. What was in the beginning, at the origin? There was the eating of the tree of life. May the Lord be merciful to us that our eyes would be opened. May we see today that we need the eating of Jesus as the tree of life. Therefore, we need to overcome not only our temper, today's fashions, or the pursuit of a doctor's degree. We need to overcome all the degraded teachings of today's Christianity.

I myself was born and raised in fundamental Christianity, and I was with the Plymouth Brethren for seven and a half years. They are very strict and famous for their teaching, and I received much knowledge from them. It took fifteen years to unload all the distracting knowledge I received from them. Today many dear hungry and seeking Christians are distracted and led away by all the teachings from the enjoyment and eating of Christ. Now the Lord is recovering us and bringing us back from all the teachings in today's degraded Christianity to the pure eating of Jesus.

RECOVERING THE CHURCH LIFE AS THE ISSUE OF THE ENJOYMENT OF CHRIST

Today the Lord is recovering the church life. We all have to realize what the church life is. The church life is the issue of the enjoyment of Christ. We cannot have a proper church life merely by teaching or gifts. In the past four or five centuries all kinds of teachings have been recovered, applied, and tested. The result has been division after division. All divisions come from different teachings. Whenever there is a great teacher, the result may be a division.

Today's Christianity has been divided mainly by two things—teachings and gifts. Today people pay attention to the charismatic things, the gifts, but many of those who emphasize the gifts are the most divisive. The charismatic groups have been divided again and again into division after division. I was in the charismatic movement for a period of time, and I received power and gifts. The real power, however, is life. Gifts and life can be compared to a thunderstorm and small flowers. A powerful thunderstorm can blow through a city, but eventually it goes away. Flowers and grass, however, continue to live and grow day by day. The church life does not need thunderstorm power; it needs life power.

The Lord's intention today is to have the recovery of the church life. The church life is a life in which day by day all the members feed on Jesus. Christ came as food to be taken in by His people. We all have to eat Jesus. Whoever takes Christ as food is a part of His Body. All the members of the Body of Christ should be the eaters of Jesus. We can be a part of Jesus only by eating Jesus. Because we eat Jesus, we become Jesus. We are members of Jesus by eating Jesus.

In 1966 the Lord gave us pray-reading. By pray-reading, many hundreds of saints have been brought into oneness. The more we pray-read, the more we are brought into oneness. If a few brothers come together only to recite and study John 1:1, after a short time they will fight. If they do not fight, they will at least be unhappy with each other. However, if these same brothers come together and pray-read, there will a different result. If I say, "Hallelujah, in the beginning!", you say, "Amen!", and two brothers say, "Was the Word!" after only ten minutes we will shout, "Oh, the sweetness! Oh, the oneness! Oh, the Spirit!"

From the beginning to the end, the Bible is a matter of eating. There is the tree of life in Genesis 2, the manna in the wilderness, and the produce of the good land. Then of the four Gospels, the Gospel of John especially reveals eating. The Lord tells us that He is the bread of life for us to eat. Eventually, in the last chapter of Revelation, there is no power, knowledge, or gifts. There is only a throne, from which a river flows, and on either side of the river is the tree of life (22:1-2). "Blessed are those who wash their robes that they may have right to the tree of life and may enter by the gates into the city" (v. 14). The eating of the tree of life is for eternity.

We need power, but this is not something for the normal daily life of the church. The church is God's cultivated land (1 Cor. 3:9). The church is a harvest, a crop. Because the church is a crop, Paul says, "I planted, Apollos watered, but God caused the growth" (v. 6). This planting, watering, and growing are all things related to life. Never forget that the church is a cultivated land, a harvest, and that all the members of the church need the growth in life. We can grow only by eating. There is no other way to grow.

EATING JESUS BY EXERCISING OUR SPIRIT
TO CONTACT HIM

From the first page to the last page of the Bible, there is

the eating of the Lord. Many know that Jesus is the bread of life, and some also know that we need to feed on Jesus, but they do not know the way to eat Him, to feed upon Him, and to be nourished by Him. How do we eat Jesus? The Jewish believers at the time the Lord Jesus spoke concerning eating Him were puzzled. They said, "How can this man give us His flesh to eat?...This word is hard; who can hear it?" (John 6:52, 60). Then the Lord Jesus said, "It is the Spirit who gives life; the flesh profits nothing" (v. 63). He seemed to be saying, "Do not consider that I am only the flesh. You have to know that one day I will become the life-giving Spirit." By being resurrected, the last Adam in the flesh was made a life-giving Spirit. Christ today is the Spirit who gives life, and this Christ is in our spirit (1 Cor. 15:45b; Rom. 8:11; 1 Cor. 6:17; 2 Tim. 4:22). The Lord is within us, in our spirit, so we must exercise our spirit to contact Him.

CALLING UPON THE NAME OF THE LORD

The proper way to contact the Lord is to call on His name: "For the same Lord is Lord of all and rich to all who call upon Him" (Rom. 10:12). Learn to call on Him. Do not be a silent Christian, that is, a dumb Christian. In 1 Corinthians 12:2-3 Paul says, "You know that when you were Gentiles, you were always being led away to dumb idols, whenever and however you were led. Therefore I make known to you that no one speaking in the Spirit of God says, Jesus is accursed; and no one can say, Jesus is Lord! except in the Holy Spirit." Formerly we were dumb worshippers, but today we are dealing with a speaking God. Therefore, we should no longer be dumb. We have to utter something. The Lord is rich unto all who call upon Him.

Suppose that during a gospel meeting, two unbelievers are inspired and become new converts. One prays in a very silent way, "Lord Jesus, I am sinful. You died on the cross for me. I believe in You. Thank You, Jesus. Amen." The other one, however, prays in a calling way, "O Lord Jesus! O Jesus!" The first one is saved, but not strongly. If we were to ask him whether or not he is saved, he may reply, "Yes, I think so." However, the second one without being asked will say, "I am saved! I may not be clear, but I know that I have joy." To call on the Lord makes a real difference. Do not think calling on the Lord is a small matter. I was a dumb Christian for many years, but one day I began to call, "O Lord Jesus!"

EATING THE WORD AS THE EMBODIMENT OF THE LIVING CHRIST

We have calling on the Lord, and we also have the Word. The Word is the embodiment of Christ. We must not consider the Bible to be a book of knowledge. If we consider the Bible as a book of knowledge, we will make it the tree of knowledge. We must consider the Bible as the embodiment of the living Christ. The Bible is the written Word, and Christ is the living Word. We must not merely exercise our mind to understand the Bible. We must exercise our spirit to eat the Bible. "Your words were found and I ate them" (Jer. 15:16).

We need to learn to eat the Word. The Word is the embodiment of the living Christ. By calling on the Lord's name and by eating His Word, we enjoy Christ. In this way we will see light, and we will also see growth and transformation. In the next chapter we will see the matter of transformation which comes out of the eating of Jesus. Transformation comes out of the nourishment.

CHAPTER SIX

TRANSFORMATION FOR THE BUILDING

Scripture Reading: Gen. 2:22; 1 Cor. 3:12a; Rev. 21:19a

EATING CHRIST AS THE TREE OF LIFE

In the previous chapter we spoke of eating Christ as the tree of life in the form of food. This is revealed in full from the very beginning of the Bible, through the whole content of the Bible, to the end of the Bible. The Bible begins with the tree of life, it continues with the tree of life, and it closes with the tree of life. The tree of life is nothing less than God in Christ presenting Himself to us as life in the form of food. We must not forget the phrase *good for food...the tree of life* in Genesis 2:9. In the Gospel of John the Lord Jesus presented Himself to people as the bread of life. John 6:35 says, "Jesus said to them, I am the bread of life; he who comes to Me shall by no means hunger, and he who believes into Me shall by no means ever thirst," and in 6:57 He said, "He who eats Me, he also shall live because of Me." At the end of the Bible there is also the tree of life (Rev. 22:2). The tree of life is our portion for eternity. For eternity we will be feeding on Jesus Christ as the tree of life. It is clear that the Bible is a book of eating. It is not a cookbook or a manual, but a table, a feast. Whenever we come to the Bible, we come to the table, the feast, for eating. Hallelujah, Jesus is the table, and Jesus is the feast! We come to Jesus and we feed on Jesus.

THE TWO ENDS OF THE BIBLE

If we pay our attention to the Bible, we will see that the two ends of the Bible correspond one with the other; they reflect each other. At the beginning of the Bible is a garden

(Gen. 2:8), and at the end of the Bible is a city (Rev. 21:10). At the beginning of the Bible are the tree of life and a river (Gen. 2:9-10), and at the end of the Bible there are also the tree of life and a river (Rev. 22:1-2). At the beginning of the Bible there is gold, bdellium (a kind of pearl), and precious stones (Gen. 2:11-12), and at the end of the Bible there are also gold, pearls, and precious stones (Rev. 21:18-21). Lastly, at the beginning of the Bible there is a bride (Gen. 2:22); God said, "It is not good for the man to be alone" (v. 18). At the end of the Bible there is also a bride (Rev. 21:2, 9). By this we can see that the two ends of the Bible reflect each other. The Bible has been in our hands for many years, but we may never have seen this. There are many wonderful, marvelous things in the Bible, but regardless of how many times we have read Genesis 2 and Revelation 21 and 22, we may not have seen these matters.

The beginning of the Bible shows us God's plan, God's "blueprint." In a book on construction there is a blueprint at the beginning of the book and a photograph of a completed building at the end. Likewise, in this divine book of God's construction there is a "blueprint" at the beginning, and at the end there is a "photograph" of God's building. In between the two ends there is a process. The process of any kind of construction is not simple. After Genesis 2, in the very first verse of chapter three, the subtle one, the serpent, came in. This serpent continues throughout the whole Bible up until Revelation 20. In the process of the divine construction, there has always been the trouble caused by this subtle one. In between Genesis 1 and 2 and Revelation 21 and 22 is the process of construction with all the distractions, all the frustrations, from the serpent. This process is a story of the subtlety of the serpent. Just before the last two chapters of the Bible, however, this serpent will be cast out (20:10). He crept in from the first verse of Genesis 3, and he will be cast out in the twentieth chapter of Revelation. This view covers the whole Bible. Today we are in the process of construction. The little serpent is here all the time, but the seed of the woman, Christ, has bruised the head of the serpent (Gen. 3:15). Praise the Lord! Regardless of how subtle the serpent is, his head has been bruised. Now he is a defeated foe who has already been cast down (Rev. 12:9).

At the two ends of the Bible there is no difference in the tree of life or the river of living water. However, the garden at the beginning of the Bible becomes a city at the end. A garden is something natural without any building. A city, however, is not natural; it is something built. In the garden the gold, pearl, and precious stones were individual pieces, but in the city the gold, pearl, and precious stones are all built into one entity. In the city there are no longer only the pieces but the building. With the bride in Genesis 2 and Revelation 21 there is also a difference. The bride in Genesis 2 is a type of the church, while the city, the New Jerusalem, is the fulfillment of the bride.

THE NEED FOR TRANSFORMATION FOR THE BUILDING

Both ends of the Bible contain many figures. These are not merely printed words; they are pictures. Therefore, we have to see their meaning. Adam was a man made of clay, the dust of the ground, but God put him in front of the tree of life. Beside the tree of life there was the flowing river, and in the flow of the river there was not clay but gold, pearl, and precious stones. Eventually at the end of Genesis 2 there is a woman as a bride, not born but built by God. This picture is very meaningful. We need the whole Bible to tell us what it signifies.

This figure signifies that man, as the dust of the ground, a piece of clay, needs to be transformed to become gold, pearl, and precious stone to be built together to become a bride. The bride at the end of the Bible is a city built with gold, pearls, and precious stones. What is needed for this is transformation. A piece of clay is not good for God's building. The buildings of the enemy, Satan, are always with brick. The tower of Babel in Genesis 11 and the two cities of Pharaoh in Exodus 1 were built with bricks made of burnt clay (vv. 11, 14). Pharaoh charged the people of Israel to gather straw and burn clay into bricks. God's building, however, is always with stone. God does not need anything muddy. God needs gold, pearls, and precious stones. In order to become these elements we have to be transformed.

BEING TRANSFORMED BY EATING CHRIST AS THE TREE OF LIFE

The way to be transformed is to take the tree of life into us, that is, to eat Christ. According to our experience, when we take Jesus into us as the tree of life, something within us starts to grow. When we take Jesus into us, we have a flow within. Now the tree of life is within us, and there is something flowing. We may have the intention to go somewhere, but something may flow within us, telling us, "Do not go. Rather, rise, pray, and get prepared for the meeting tonight." We have such a flow within us. The more it flows, the more life we have, and the "muddy" things within are transformed into something golden. If we are still "muddy," we need more flowing. When we call, "O Lord Jesus," there is a flow within us.

We receive the flowing not by teaching but by eating Jesus. When we eat Jesus, we have the river of life within. In John 6:57 Jesus said, "He who eats Me, he also shall live because of Me," and in 7:38 He said, "He who believes into Me, as the Scripture said, out of his innermost being shall flow rivers of living water." In John 6 there is the eating, and in chapter seven there is the flowing. When the tree of life gets into us, it becomes the river. This river flows within us, and this flow transforms us into gold, pearls, and precious stones. We all have to say, "Hallelujah for the transformation! We are not only regenerated, but we are also being transformed."

We are not fully transformed yet. A brother may like to play basketball, but by transformation by the flowing of the life of Christ, his playing of basketball will cease. In Los Angeles in the past few years a number of hippies came to our meeting. Night after night one such person would come with long hair, a beard, and bare feet to sit on the front row. Another came wearing a dirty blanket-like garment. A dear saint warned me at that time that the church was in danger of becoming a "hippy church." I told this one simply to wait; the Lord would work everything out. Still, after several days and weeks I did expect to see that the brother would put away that blanket. This was a real test to me. Hallelujah, after a few months he did put away his blanket. Moreover, the brother with the long hair was cleanly shaven. When he walked into the meeting like this, everyone shouted for joy. However, his feet were still bare. For several more weeks I was still under the test. I was tempted to give a message on dressing properly, but the Lord said within me, "Do not do it. Do not trust in teaching. Trust in Me. Trust in the flowing, the watering life, the transforming life." After not too long, this brother put on a pair of good shoes. This was transformation. Praise the Lord, we do have a transforming life.

BEING TURNED FROM TEACHINGS AND GIFTS TO CHRIST AS FOOD

The Lord has burdened us with the revelation that teachings can never build up the church. Neither do gifts work. Only Christ as life can build the church. Teachings help us to realize that we need Christ as life, and good, proper teachings minister Christ to us as life. But teachings alone do not work. We all need Christ, not Christ in doctrine, but the living Christ as the life-giving Spirit. The Christ who is the Spirit really works. Likewise, gifts are good, but gifts are a means, a utensil, to help people to have a realization of Christ. Gifts are not Christ. Gifts help us to take Christ, but if we substitute the gifts for Christ, we are wrong. We have to eat Christ. However, the tragedy today is that people pay attention to the gifts much more than to Christ. We all have to be turned from teachings to Christ, and we all have to be turned from gifts to Christ. Christ—and Christ alone—is the substance, the element, and all the ingredients of the spiritual food, so we have to take Christ.

Christ is the tree of life. The more we take Christ in, the more we have the flow within. If we say, "O Lord Jesus," ten times, there will be the flow of the living water within us. Then we should pick up the Bible, open to any page, and pray-read a few verses. We should not merely exercise our mind to understand the Bible; we must exercise our spirit to pray the Bible. By praying we take the Word, we eat the Word.

I assure you that if you call on the Lord and pray-read like this in the morning, something will be flowing within you and watering you, and along with this flowing there will be the nourishing, enlightening, strengthening, comforting, regulating, and saturating. This will cause you to be transformed. The church is built up by this transformation.

We are men of clay. Regardless of whether we are low class, middle class, or high class, whether we have a Ph.D. or have no education, we all are pieces of clay, not good for the building up of the church. We are "muddy." Regardless of whether we are barbarian or Scythian, circumcision or uncircumcision, bond or free, great or small, whether we are hippies on the street or we wear a tie, we are still pieces of clay. If we build a building with clay and a storm comes, the building will become a marsh. There are too many marshes in the United States today. A marsh is neither dry land or a flowing river. However, the more flow we have, the more the clay will be discharged, and we will be transformed day by day.

THE INWARD TRANSFORMATION IN LIFE

We were made a tripartite being. First Thessalonians 5:23 tells us that we are persons of three parts—spirit, soul, and body. One day when we opened up ourselves and called on the name of the Lord, He came in. By calling, "O Lord Jesus," we gave Him an invitation. He took the invitation, He came into us, and we were regenerated. Our sins were washed away by His blood, and He came in not only as the Savior, the Redeemer, and the Lord, but also as the life-giving Spirit. First Corinthians 15:45b says, "The last Adam became a life-giving Spirit." He is the Spirit in our spirit, so we are one spirit with Him, as 1 Corinthians 6:17 says, "He who is joined to the Lord is one spirit." We are here as one spirit with the Lord.

However, we must also consider our soul. Our soul is composed mainly of the mind. We should not love our mind. Our mind is a real troublemaker. Whenever we exercise our mind, we have trouble. There is no need to try to be in the mind. As soon as we wake up, we may have a critical thought about our spouse. Right away we have to say, "O Lord Jesus!" and get ourselves out of our mind and misery. Do not stay in the mind, but turn from the mind to the spirit. The mind, emotion, and will are awful things. It is so easy to be irritated in our emotions. If a brother is told he is nice, he will feel happy, but if he is corrected, his countenance will fall. Just by one sentence we can be made to laugh or be angry. The emotions are so fragile. Likewise, the will is so stubborn. It is wonderful that Jesus is in our spirit, but He may not be in our mind, emotion, and will.

Mere outward change, outward correction, means nothing. Many Christians like to talk about sanctification. To be sanctified is not merely to be sinless. The Brethren taught that to be sanctified is to be separated from what is common. In a sense this is right, but this is a positional change. We must realize that a positional change alone does not mean much. Regardless of the position of our troublesome mind, terrible emotion, and stubborn will, they are still a problem. We need a dispositional change. We need transformation. Transformation is a "chemical" change, a change in nature and element. Our awful mind needs a wonderful element to get into it. For a chemical change to take place, one element must be put into another. Without Christ getting into our mind, our mind can never have a "chemical" change. We can have a change in our thinking, a change in our concept, but our mind will still remain the same in nature. We need a "chemical" change in our mind. This means that Christ as the heavenly element must get into our mind. When Christ gets into our mind, the mind is renewed; it is transformed. This is the clay being transformed into gold, pearl, and precious stone. This is not outward correction or outward adjustment, but the inward transformation in life by another element. This is why we have to be filled in our spirit (Eph. 5:18) and say, "O Lord!" Whenever we say, "O Lord," the Lord gets into us, and we are filled in our spirit unto the fullness of God. We are filled with all that God is in Christ.

TRANSFORMATION MAKING US QUALIFIED FOR THE BUILDING

If we have the infilling in our spirit, we surely will have the outflow into our mind. This outflow will saturate our mind and emotion. This is not correction from without but saturation from within. This is the real change, a change in nature, a change in disposition, and this is the proper, subjective sanctification. Originally our mind, emotion, and will were muddy, but now our mind is becoming gold, our emotion is becoming pearl, and our will is becoming precious stone. By this we are qualified, we are just right, for the building.

Here in this country in the past few years, by God's mercy we have seen the gold, the pearls, and the precious stones. Many who have visited the church in Los Angeles have testified that the most striking, inspiring, and convincing point there is the eating of Christ. Sometimes several hundred people meet together, but no hint of differing opinions can be found among them. The oneness is there because the muddy mind has been swallowed up by the presence of Jesus, the terrible emotion has been transformed by the element of Christ, and the stubborn will also has been transformed. This is just right for the building. For the church in your locality to be thoroughly built up, all the dear ones must pay their full attention to the eating of Christ. Do not care for mere teachings. Rather, eat Christ, call on the Lord, breathe Him in, and eat the Word by pray-reading. If we do this, we will have the real gifts. Some people ask us if we have the gifts in our meeting. Actually, there are many gifts in the meeting. We all have to realize that the main thing that we need to build up a local church is to take Jesus as our life—to eat Him, to drink of Him, and to breathe Him in. Then all the pieces of clay will be transformed.

THE OPERATION OF THE TRIUNE GOD
FOR OUR TRANSFORMATION

In Genesis 2 there are three kinds of precious materials, which match the three of the Triune God. Gold refers to the divine nature of the Father. The more we call on the Lord Jesus and enjoy Christ, the more gold we have. This means that we participate in the divine nature. The more we enjoy Christ, the more of the divine nature we have. Pearls refer to Christ with His redemptive work on the cross. A pearl comes out of an oyster. When a grain of sand wounds the oyster and remains in the wound, the oyster secretes its life-juice around the grain of sand. In this way the grain of sand becomes a pearl. Christ is the living oyster who came into the death water, and we are the grains of sand who wounded Him. As we remain in the church, His life-juice continually secretes over us to make us into precious pearls. The more we enjoy Christ, the more we stay with Him, the more we enjoy the secretion of His life-juice. Precious stones are not created but are produced by the transforming of things already created. This refers to the work of the Holy Spirit. As the Holy Spirit burns us and presses us, we, the created matter, become precious stones. Gold, pearls, and precious stones denote the working of the Father, the Son, and the Holy Spirit. This operation makes us fit for the building of the Lord.

Brothers and sisters, we all need such a transformation. It is not teachings that build up the church. Neither are the gifts adequate to build up the Body. Rather, it is the transforming life of the living Christ. Let us all turn ourselves to the living Christ. Turn to Christ from teachings. Turn to Christ from the gifts. We must never take the Bible as a book of theology or a book of knowledge. We must take it as a book of life, as the embodiment of the living Christ, as the Spirit. In this way we enjoy Christ, and we eat Him, drink Him, and breathe Him in. If we do this, we will have the transformation.

Those who are trying to do a work merely by teaching others will get nothing. Whatever they do will be in vain. We all have to minister Christ to others. We may use teachings as the means, but we do not minister teachings to others. We minister Christ to others by helping them to eat Christ in the teachings. Likewise, do not help people to have the gifts. Gifts help people, but what people need is not the gifts but Christ. Learn to enjoy Christ. Learn to experience Christ. Learn to participate in Christ. Then learn to minister the Christ whom you have experienced to others. This will not only cause people to be regenerated in their spirit, but also will cause them to be transformed in their soul. It by this transformation that people will be ready for the building. Praise the Lord, the local churches are built up in this way.

CHAPTER SEVEN

THE ENJOYMENT OF CHRIST
IN 1 CORINTHIANS

Scripture Reading: 1 Cor. 1:30; 12:3; 1:2, 9, 22-23

EATING JESUS BEING
THE BASIC CONCEPT IN THE BIBLE

As we have seen in previous chapters, from the beginning to the end of the Bible the main, central, and basic concept of God is that we must eat Jesus. After God created man, He put him in front of the tree of life, indicating that man should eat the tree of life. When the Lord Jesus came, He presented Himself to us as the bread of life (John 6:35). He said, "He who eats Me, he also shall live because of Me" (v. 57). This word is very strong, definite, and clear. However, most of us never heard a message in Christianity which told us that we need to eat Jesus. Therefore, we should not trust the teachings in Christianity that miss the basic concept in the Bible.

The matter of eating is mentioned again and again in the Bible. Nothing is more basic than eating. At the Passover the people ate the meat of the lamb and the unleavened bread (Exo. 12:3, 8, 15). In the wilderness the people ate manna day by day (16:4, 35). Then at the end of the Bible, in the book of Revelation, the tree of life is mentioned again: "To him who overcomes, to him I will give to eat of the tree of life, which is in the Paradise of God" (Rev. 2:7). Also Revelation 22:14 says, "Blessed are those who wash their robes that they may have right to the tree of life." For eternity our portion is to eat Jesus as the tree of life.

THE BASIC CONCEPT OF 1 CORINTHIANS

In order to understand any verse of the Bible we must always take care of its context. The context includes both the chapter as well as the entire book. Here we will present the basic concept of the book of 1 Corinthians. The fundamentalists and the Pentecostals have misused or overemphasized certain verses in this book. It is dreadful to misuse the Word. Still, I have no intention to argue with anyone. Rather, my burden from the Lord is to show His people the proper concept in the Word.

The Plymouth Brethren, who published a number of books on 1 Corinthians, mainly pointed out the teachings used to solve some of the problems of the church in Corinth. These problems include marriage, the Lord's table, head covering, and lawsuits between brothers. The Brethren emphasized the teachings in 1 Corinthians. They used verse 26 of chapter fourteen, for example, to show in a doctrinal way how to meet. In contrast to the Brethren, the Pentecostals mainly emphasize chapter twelve and other verses of chapter fourteen.

We must come back to the pure Word according to the whole context and full scope of 1 Corinthians. In order to find a street in a city, you have to look at the whole city. Then you will know which direction to take in order to find a certain street. If we look into the entire scope of 1 Corinthians, we will know where chapters twelve and fourteen stand, and we will also know how the problems mentioned in 1 Corinthians can be solved.

PAUL'S GREETING
TO THE CHURCH OF GOD IN CORINTH

Each book of the Bible has its particular beginning. Genesis begins with, "In the beginning God created the heavens and the earth." Matthew begins with "The book of the generation of Jesus Christ, the son of David, the son of Abraham." John begins with, "In the beginning was the Word, and the Word was with God, and the Word was God." First Corinthians begins in a special way: "Paul, a called apostle of Christ Jesus through the will of God, and Sosthenes the brother, to the church of God which is in Corinth, to those who have been sanctified in Christ Jesus, the called saints, with all those who call upon the name of our Lord Jesus Christ in every place, who is theirs and ours" (1:1-2). This greeting is unique among all the sixty-six books of the Bible. If I had been Paul, I might have been very simple, addressing my letter with, "To the brothers and sisters in Corinth" or "To the Corinthian believers." Paul's address, however, is very complicated, having at least seven points. First he says, "to the church"; second, "of God"; third, "which is in Corinth"; fourth, "to those who have been sanctified in Christ Jesus"; fifth, "the called saints"; sixth, "with all those who call upon the name of our Lord Jesus Christ"; and seventh, "who is theirs and ours."

We need at least one message for each of these seven points. The phrase *which is in Corinth* is a special phrase. It does not say that the church is in the heavens or in the air. It says that the church is in Corinth. This means that the church is something in a locality; in Corinth there is a local church. What is the meaning of the phrase *sanctified in Christ Jesus,* and what is the meaning of *called saints*? We are not called to be saints, as the King James Version says. We are already called, not as sinners, publicans, teachers, or scholars, but as saints.

THE CALLED SAINTS
CALLING UPON THE NAME OF THE LORD

In verse 2 there are two kinds of calling. First we have been called by the Lord; then we have to call upon the name of our Lord Jesus Christ. We are the called ones, and we are also the calling ones. We have been called to call on Him. He has called us, and now we call upon Him. This is a two-way traffic. We are the calling ones based upon our standing that we are the called ones. If we were not the called ones, we could never be the calling ones.

The Christ we call upon is "theirs and ours." This Christ is mine, and this Christ is yours. If I say, "Christ is mine," you have to say, "Christ is mine too!" This is very meaningful. We should underline this phrase in verse 2. This is the only place in the entire Bible that such a phrase appears. The books of Ephesians and Romans are wonderful and excellent, but neither of these two books has the phrase *theirs and ours.*

CALLED BY GOD INTO THE FELLOWSHIP
OF HIS SON, JESUS CHRIST

Christ is our portion, and we have been called by God into the fellowship of this portion. First Corinthians 1:9 says, "God is faithful, through whom you were called into the fellowship of His Son, Jesus Christ our Lord." God, the faithful One, has called us into the fellowship of His Son. He did not call us into "mansions" in heaven, into knowledge or teaching, into the doctrines and teachings of Christ, into the manifestation of the gifts, or into the baptism of the Spirit. He has called us into the fellowship of His Son.

THE SIGN-SEEKING JEWS
AND THE WISDOM-SEEKING GREEKS

Verse 22 of chapter one says, "For indeed Jews require signs and Greeks seek wisdom." A sign is something miraculous. Because the Jews believe in God, they often think that He is a miracle-performing God. When the Jews came to the Lord Jesus, they said, "What sign then will You do that we may see and believe You? What work will You do? Our fathers ate the manna in the wilderness, as it is written, 'He gave them bread out of heaven to eat'" (John 6:30-31). The Jews challenged the Lord Jesus. For forty years in the wilderness they had a miracle every day. That was not a small miracle. Today, if a number of people would quit their jobs and trust in the Lord, and manna would come down every morning for them, all the newspapers would publish this miracle. The ancient Jews enjoyed such a miracle every day for forty years; yet they were not edified. Their response to God was to murmur and complain (Num. 11:1). This is strong proof that the miraculous things do not edify anyone.

John 2:23 says, "Now when He was in Jerusalem at the Passover, during the feast, many believed into His name when they saw the signs which He did." This may seem to be wonderful, but verse 24 says, "But Jesus Himself did not entrust

Himself to them, for He knew all men." If we believe in Jesus because of the miracles we have seen, Jesus will not believe in us. Many of the Jews believed in Jesus because of the miracles, but Jesus would not entrust Himself to them. The Lord knew that those who came to Him by miracles were not trustworthy.

The Jews require signs, but the Greeks seek after wisdom. Signs are a matter of gifts, while wisdom refers to knowledge or teaching. Today in Christianity there are still these two categories of people. Some are "Christian Jews" requiring miracles; others are "Christian Greeks" seeking after wisdom and a Ph.D. in the knowledge of the Bible.

CHRIST CRUCIFIED

The Jews require signs and the Greeks seek wisdom, but "we preach Christ crucified" (1 Cor. 1:23). Apparently, there was no power in Christ's crucifixion. When Jesus was arrested, He did not perform a miracle to save Himself. That night and the next day He was brought to six stations—three related to the priests and three to the Roman government—yet He did not resist. Eventually He was sentenced, brought to Calvary, and nailed on the cross. He did not do anything miraculous; apparently He was weak to the uttermost. If we had been there, we might have struggled, doing whatever we could to resist. However, Jesus did nothing. He was crucified out of weakness (2 Cor. 13:4).

Paul preached Christ crucified. This kind of Christ was a stumbling block to the Jews who require signs. The Jews might say, "Our God is a God of miracles. How can the Messiah of God be crucified? We cannot believe in such a Messiah. This surely cannot be the Messiah from God." To the Jews such a Christ was a stumbling block.

To the Greeks the crucified Christ was foolishness. There was no wisdom in such a thing. They thought that if Christ were wise, He surely should have escaped. Thus, Christ crucified was foolishness to them. Yet Paul said, "But to those who are called, both Jews and Greeks, Christ the power of God and the wisdom of God" (1 Cor. 1:24).

CHRIST AS WISDOM TO US FROM GOD

Christ is the wisdom of God. First Corinthians 1:30 says, "But of Him you are in Christ Jesus, who became wisdom to us from God: both righteousness and sanctification and redemption." Hallelujah, we are in Christ Jesus! It is of God that we are in Christ. We were not born in Him, but we were made to be in Him. Christ was made wisdom to us from God as three items: righteousness, sanctification, and redemption. Righteousness is for our past, sanctification is for our present, and redemption is for our future.

Christ as Our Righteousness for Our Past

As an older person, I dare not look at my past. Even a young man of twenty years of age realizes that his short past is terrible. None of us has a good past. Because our past is awful, we need Christ as our righteousness. This is the real remedy, the real cure. Hallelujah, we have Christ as our righteousness for our past! Now we should no longer say that our past is awful. We can say, "Our past is glorious, because our past is Christ." Formerly, our past was awful because of our wrongdoings, but now it is glorious because of Christ. Christ is our righteousness.

Christ as Our Sanctification for Our Present

Our past is glorious, but what about our present? Christ is our righteousness for our past, and Christ is our sanctification for our present. Sometimes our present is awful, but we have to say, "Hallelujah, I have Christ as my sanctification!" Sanctification is more than holiness; it is holiness "to us," not in a doctrinal way, but in a subjective and experiential way. Whereas holiness is the thing itself, sanctification is holiness becoming our experience. It is not something objective but something very personal and subjective to us. Christ is our sanctification.

Suppose a brother has a wife who gives him a hard time, irritating him, humiliating him, and causing him to lose his temper. What should he do? The teaching of fundamental Christianity would tell him that he must love his wife.

Perhaps on his wedding day he was told by his pastor that he must love his wife according to Ephesians 5:25. In his hard circumstance, he may exercise his mind to remember to love his wife. However, this does not work. He should not try to remember this teaching. When his wife gives him a hard time, he should call, "O Lord Jesus." This is to enjoy Christ, apply Christ, and appropriate Christ in our situations. Many of us can testify that this truly works. In this way Christ becomes our sanctification. Instead of losing our temper we gain Christ as our holiness in a subjective way. Sanctification is Christ becoming holiness in our experience.

Among Christians today there is much talk about sanctification. However, sanctification is a person—Jesus Christ—to be experienced today. Whenever we experience Christ today, that is a part of our sanctification. Sanctification includes many things. According to the present trend of this age, very few women can overcome the department stores. As they look in the windows and at the showcases, they get captured, and eventually they buy some of the up-to-date fashions. Then when they wear them, they lose their sanctification; instead of experiencing sanctification they experience worldliness. What should the sisters do? As a sister looks at the show windows of the department stores, she should call, "O Lord Jesus." Even if she is already at the counter, it is not too late. She can still say, "O Lord Jesus." This may cause her to leave what she has picked up. Then if she continues to call, the Lord within her may tell her to go home and forget about the store. In such a way she will experience Christ as her daily and hourly sanctification. This is not a mere doctrine; this is Jesus as our personal sanctification.

Many young men today like to have long hair. If a brother has long hair, do you believe that people will realize that Christ is his sanctification? I do not believe so. Some long-haired Christians today call themselves "Jesus People." However, these people of Jesus are not wearing Jesus; they are wearing their long hair. If a young man with long hair calls, "O Lord Jesus," as he combs his hair, the Lord Jesus may say, "Cut it." Even the length of our hair is not a matter of regulation or outward correction; it is a matter of sanctification.

Jesus Christ should be our haircut. This is the experience of sanctification in all matters.

Many Christians today are poor because they have the doctrines, but nothing is effective. They have the gifts, but there is no change in life. Day by day, we need to experience Christ as our sanctification. Every aspect of our daily walk must be Christ. Our haircut must be Christ. Our shopping must be Christ. Our clothing must be Christ. Our attitude must be Christ. Our relationship with our family must be Christ. Even the pair of shoes we wear must be Christ. In this way Christ becomes prevailing in our daily walk. This is the experience of life with Christ as our daily sanctification. Thus, we are sanctified, separated, marked out, and absolutely different from the worldly people. Our shopping and our clothing must be different from that of the worldly people. This is not merely my teaching; it is our experience of Christ as our daily holiness.

Christ as Our Redemption for Our Future

Christ is also for our future. Some day He will come, and we will be transfigured. That will be the redemption of our body (Rom. 8:23; Phil. 3:21).

CHRIST AS THE LAST ADAM
BECOMING THE LIFE-GIVING SPIRIT

We have been called into the fellowship of Jesus Christ. Fellowship means participation or enjoyment. Therefore, we have been called into the participation and enjoyment of Christ. Day by day, we fellowship with this Christ, we enjoy this Christ, and we participate in this Christ. Never forget that this Christ is the last Adam who became a life-giving Spirit (1 Cor. 15:45b). Many have heard much about the Holy Spirit, the baptism of the Holy Spirit, and the gifts of the Holy Spirit, but few have heard that Christ today is the life-giving Spirit. This is why we say that we should not trust the teachings in Christianity that miss the basic concept in the Bible.

The Holy Spirit and the gifts of the Holy Spirit are facts, but 1 Corinthians 15:45b is also a fact. Christ today is a life-giving Spirit. This is not my word, nor is it merely my teaching; this is 1 Corinthians 15:45b: "The last Adam became a life-giving Spirit." The Christ who was made wisdom to us from God as our righteousness for our past, as our sanctification for our present, and as our redemption for our future is the life-giving Spirit today. If He were not the life-giving Spirit today, He could not be our righteousness or our sanctification. If He were not such a life-giving Spirit who lives within us, how could He be so subjective to us? He would remain who He is, and we would remain who we are. He would have nothing to do with us, and we would not be related to Him. Praise Him, He is the life-giving Spirit! At the time we called on Him, saying, "O Lord Jesus," whether or not we had the knowledge, He entered into us. Yes, He is in the heavens, but hallelujah, He is also in us! He is not only the Lamb of God, the Redeemer, the Savior, and the Lord; He is also the life-giving Spirit. "And the Lord is the Spirit" (2 Cor. 3:17). Now the Lord Jesus is the life-giving Spirit, and as the life-giving Spirit He is in us.

Today most Christians appreciate John 3:16, but we need to appreciate 1 Corinthians 15:45 more. Yet, even John 3:16 implies that Christ is the life-giving Spirit. It says, "For God so loved the world that He gave His only begotten Son, that every one who believes into Him would not perish, but would have eternal life." God has given His Son to us. Where is His Son today? Without having Jesus within us, how could we have eternal life? Eternal life is simply Jesus Himself. We have eternal life because we have Jesus. God has given Him to us, and we have received Him. Now we have Him within us, so we have Jesus Himself as the eternal life. Jesus can be eternal life to us because He is within us as the life-giving Spirit. Because Jesus today is the life-giving Spirit living within us, He is everything to us.

In Indianapolis in 1968, as a brother drove me to a meeting, he said, "Brother Lee, in this country people always tell others to look to the Lord who is in the heavens while we are on earth. However, you always tell people to turn to their spirit. This seems to be a different direction." He warned me that some people were saying that this is an oriental philosophy. Earlier that same evening I had received an impression from the Lord that I should say something in the meeting about Christ being within us. After we sang and prayed in the meeting, I picked up the Bible and read Romans 8. In my speaking, I pointed out that chapter eight has two key verses concerning where Christ is. Verse 34 says that Christ is in the heavens, while verse 10 says that Christ is in us. I then asked the listeners, "Where is Christ today? In the heavens or in you?" Using the illustration of electricity, I told them that this is an easy question to answer. The same electricity is both in the generator and in the meeting hall. As long as electricity has been installed, whenever we need it, we should not look to the generator; we should simply go to the switch and turn it on. I then asked the listeners, "Is this oriental philosophy? No, it is not. Christ as the heavenly electricity has been installed in our spirit. When we need to apply Him, should we look to the heavens or should we turn to our spirit?" To be sure, we should turn and exercise our spirit to "switch on" by saying, "O Lord Jesus."

Another wonderful verse is 1 Corinthians 6:17, which says, "He who is joined to the Lord is one spirit." Now we should exercise our spirit. After electricity has been installed in a building, we simply go and turn on the switch. Likewise, the wonderful and marvelous Christ has been installed in our spirit (2 Tim. 4:22). Therefore, we simply need to turn to our spirit.

This is not merely my teaching; this is the divine revelation in the book of 1 Corinthians. Again I say, Christianity has missed the mark. We may have read many messages on 1 Corinthians, but not one of them told us that Christ today is the life-giving Spirit within us. Not one of them told us that we must exercise our spirit. Yet this is the basic concept of 1 Corinthians.

First Corinthians 16:18 says, "For they refreshed my spirit and yours," and 2 Corinthians 7:13 says, "His spirit has been refreshed by all of you." This shows us that our Christian life and walk is in our spirit. This is because Christ is in our spirit.

EXERCISING OUR SPIRIT BY CALLING ON THE LORD

First Corinthians tells us that we all have been called into the fellowship, the participation, of this Christ, who is now the life-giving Spirit. He has been made our righteousness for the past, our sanctification for the present, and our redemption for the future. We are one with Him as the life-giving Spirit in our spirit. Now we must call on Him (1 Cor. 12:3; Rom. 10:12). We should not merely pray to Him or ask Him, but call on Him. Praying and asking may be illustrated by speaking something in a soft and low voice. Calling, however, may be compared to crying, "Please help me!" To speak in this way is not only to ask or to pray; it is to call. If I were to report that a house is on fire, I would not say in a soft tone of voice, "Brother, the house is on fire. Could you come and help us?" This may be compared to praying or asking. To call, however, is like shouting, "Fire! Fire!" There is a big difference. We should try to call in this way.

When a house is on fire, no man tries to be a gentleman, and no woman tries to be a lady. In order to be rescued, they must call desperately. Similarly, when our spouse gives us a hard time, we may pray, "Lord, help me not to lose my temper," but eventually we may lose it. Rather, we need to be rescued. By calling, "O Lord Jesus," our temper will be consumed, and immediately we will be rescued.

APPLYING CHRIST BY EXERCISING OUR SPIRIT

In 1 Corinthians 2:14 Paul says, "But a soulish man does not receive the things of the Spirit of God, for they are foolishness to him and he is not able to know them because they are discerned spiritually." In order to know the things of the Spirit of God, we must not exercise our natural mind or our soul. This is the wrong organ. If we exercise our soul, we will be insulated from Christ as the electricity. Even a small thing, such as a thin piece of paper, can insulate electricity. We must forget about our natural mind and simply turn to our spirit. Paul said that only the spiritual ones can discern the things of the Spirit. Christ is the life-giving Spirit in our spirit, and we are one spirit with Him in our spirit. Whenever we need Him, our only way is to apply Him by exercising our spirit.

CHAPTER EIGHT

EATING, DRINKING, GROWING, TRANSFORMATION, AND BUILDING

Scripture Reading: 1 Cor. 3:2; 5:7b-8; 10:3-4, 16-18, 21; 11:23-25; 12:13b, 3b; 3:6, 9b, 12a

From the verses in the Scripture reading above we can see the unique matters of eating, drinking, growing, transformation, and building. The word *transformed* is used in 2 Corinthians 3:18, which says, "But we all with unveiled face, beholding and reflecting like a mirror the glory of the Lord, are being transformed into the same image from glory to glory, even as from the Lord Spirit." Transformation is also indicated in 1 Corinthians 3:9 and 12. Verse 9 says, "For we are God's fellow workers; you are God's cultivated land, God's building." Verse 12 says, "But if anyone builds upon the foundation gold, silver, precious stones, wood, grass, stubble." A farm is not a mine; a farm is for growing plants. But in verse 12 we do not have plants; we have gold, silver, and precious stones which are good for building. The farm grows plants, yet eventually we have precious stones. This indicates transformation. Transformation may also be illustrated by petrified wood. Petrified wood is from trees that have become stone.

The matters of eating, drinking, growing, transformation, and building are not merely our teaching. They are the revelation in 1 Corinthians. Many in Christianity often refer to 1 Corinthians. The Brethren published books dealing with the eleven problems in this book. The first of the eleven problems is the problem of division (1:10—4:21). Some said they were of Paul, some were of Apollos, some of Cephas, and some said they were of Christ (1:12). To this Paul said, "Is Christ divided?" (v. 13). Secondly, this book deals with the excommunication of an evil brother (5:1-13). A sinful brother committed incest with his stepmother, so Paul told the Corinthians to remove the evil man from among them (v. 13). In chapter six is the dealing with lawsuits among believers (6:1-11) and dealing with the abuse of freedom (6:12-20). In chapter seven is the dealing with marriage life (7:1-40). Following this is the dealing with the eating of things sacrificed to idols (8:1—11:1) with the vindication of Paul's apostleship and authority (9:1-27). In chapter eleven are the matters of head covering (11:2-16) and the Lord's supper (11:17-34). Then in 12:1—14:40 is the dealing with the gifts. Lastly are the dealings with the matter of resurrection (15:1-58) and the collection of the gift (16:1-9).

According to teaching, the Brethren were right, and we have come to know their teachings very well, but I have the burden to convince you that teachings alone are not sufficient. We ourselves can publish many books on the eleven problems in 1 Corinthians. Just on the matters of division and excommunication there are many things to say. However, what would be the use of mere knowledge about these things? None of these problems is the central concept of this book. The central concept, on the negative side, is that the Corinthians were sick with all these problems. This sickness was due to their emphasis on knowledge and the gifts. They were sick with divisions, sinfulness, lawsuits, wrongness toward marriage, idol sacrifices, and many matters. On the one hand, this is because they had too much teaching, too much knowledge. Knowledge puffs up (8:1). Likewise, they overemphasized and misused the gifts.

On the other hand, however, the Corinthians were short of the eating and enjoying of Christ. Medical doctors today tell us that certain sicknesses are due to the shortage of vitamins. The best cure for these sicknesses is not to take medicine but to take the proper vitamins. Some diseases, however, require an antibiotic, a germicide to kill the germs. In 1 Corinthians Christ is the real vitamin, and the cross is the real germicide, the antibiotic. Paul said, "For I did not determine to know anything among you except Christ, and this One crucified"

(2:2). The Corinthians were sick with many divisions because they were short of the proper "vitamins." To feed a patient quickly, doctors may feed him intravenously. When a patient is brought into a hospital in serious condition, he is fed through the veins. Then after a few days, he can be fed through the mouth. The main thing the doctors care for is the feeding. In this book Paul was feeding the Corinthians. The best cure for problems is eating.

Regrettably, both the fundamentalists and the Pentecostals have not seen the crucial matters in 1 Corinthians. It is hard to hear a message in Christianity telling us that 1 Corinthians is for eating, drinking, growing, transforming, and building. Rather, all the messages from this book are on teaching, doctrine, gifts, and the manifestation of gifts. The King James Version translates *build* as *edify* in 1 Corinthians 14 (vv. 3-5). In Greek, *edify* means to build; it is the verbal form of the noun for *house*. However, most people do not understand it in this way. Not many speak of building up. Many say that to speak in tongues edifies them. As long as they are edified, they are satisfied. Speaking in tongues may edify the speaker, but it does not build up the church (vv. 4-5).

EATING AND DRINKING IN 1 CORINTHIANS

In 1 Corinthians there are many verses dealing with the matter of eating and drinking. First Corinthians 5:8 says, "So then let us keep the feast." A feast is not an ordinary meal such as breakfast. A feast is a specially prepared meal. Verse 21 of chapter ten also speaks of the Lord's table. We should underline the verses in the Bible related to eating the Lord. The words *feast* and *table* should stand out. We keep the feast, and we partake of the Lord's table. Verses 3 and 4 say, "And all ate the same spiritual food, and all drank the same spiritual drink," and 12:13 says, "We were all...given to drink one Spirit." Many charismatic Christians speak much about the baptism in the Spirit. Baptism is to put people into the water, but to drink is to put the water into them. Baptism is outward, while drinking is inward. Today's Christianity comes short in that many talk about baptism, but they neglect the drinking. First Corinthians 12:13 covers both aspects. The first part of this verse says that we all were baptized in one Spirit. Then the second part says that we all were made to drink one Spirit. In between these two phrases is the conjunction *and,* indicating that these are two different things. To be baptized in the Spirit is one thing, while to drink the Spirit is another.

Early in the morning, I like to take a shower, and after my shower I like to sit down to take a cup of milk or tea. It is not the case that as long as I have taken a shower, I do not need to drink. This is foolish. If I had to choose between the two, I would forget about the shower, and I would sit down to drink. It may be all right to go for several days without taking a shower, but it is not all right to go without drinking. Would you rather bathe twice a day but never drink, or go without bathing but drink several times a day? My heart aches for the foolishness of today's Christianity. Many Christians do not understand what they are speaking about. As a small servant of the Lord, I must be faithful to say this; if I do not, I will cheat you. If we are honest and fair when we read 1 Corinthians, we will see the matter of eating.

PAUL'S BALANCING AND RESTRICTING OF THE GIFTS

Paul's Epistle takes a negative attitude toward the gifts. His word concerning the gifts is not encouraging toward them but balancing. In this book Paul had no intention to encourage the Corinthians to value these gifts. Rather, his burden was to balance and restrict them. The Corinthians overemphasized and overused the gifts. Many charismatic Christians quote 14:18 in which Paul says, "I thank God, I speak in tongues more than all of you," but they do not quote the following verse: "But in the church I would rather speak five words with my mind, that I might instruct others also, than ten thousand words in a tongue" (v. 19). Paul's intention was not to encourage them to use the gifts, but to restrict and balance them. Paul did not say that the gifts were wrong, but he did restrict them. Paul said, "If therefore the whole church comes together in one place, and all speak in tongues, and some unlearned in tongues or unbelievers enter, will they not say that you are insane?" (v. 23). We must be honest to say that this is not encouragement but balance. Paul goes on to say, "But if all prophesy and some unbeliever or unlearned person enters, he is convicted by all, he is examined by all" (v. 24). In this book, Paul's intention is to restrict, to balance, the gifts with the matters of eating Christ, drinking the Spirit, growing, transformation, and building.

GROWING BY FEEDING

Before this time we may never have seen the many verses in this book about eating. Paul said, "I gave you milk to drink" (3:2). He did not merely teach them but fed them. What Paul did was a feeding, not a teaching. We must enter into the spirit of the writer of this book. The spirit of this book is that the Corinthians needed the feeding. They needed eating, the proper food, not knowledge, skills, or gifts. Mothers know that the way to help their children to grow is not by teaching them but by feeding them three or more times a day. Little babies need many meals a day. If we feed children, they grow. This was exactly what Paul was doing in this book. Paul, as a spiritual mother, was feeding his children.

FEASTING BY EATING CHRIST

Paul went on to say that Christ is our Passover (5:7). The Passover has two aspects: the aspect of the blood for redemption and the aspect of the meat for eating (Exo. 12:3-10). At the Passover, the people of Israel firstly sprinkled the blood on the doorposts of their houses. After sprinkling the doorposts with the blood, they did not fast and pray; rather, they began to eat. The sprinkling is for the eating, and the eating is for walking out (vv. 11, 31). How could the Israelites leave Egypt? It was not only by the sprinkling of the blood but by the eating of the lamb. By their eating they had the strength to leave Egypt. In the past I heard many messages in Christianity about the sprinkling of the blood, but I did not hear a message about the eating of the lamb. Paul said that Christ is our Passover, not only for redeeming but also for feeding. He shed His blood for redeeming; now He affords Himself for feeding. We all have to feed on Jesus. We have to eat the Lamb with the unleavened bread.

Paul said, "So then let us keep the feast" (1 Cor. 5:8). After the Passover we enter into the feast. Day by day we are feasting on the unleavened bread. Bible students agree that the unleavened bread in typology is Christ. Therefore, we are feasting by eating Christ as the unleavened bread. This is the spirit of the writer of this book. Do not bring your own concept into this book. You have to drop your concept and get into the spirit of the writer. The spirit of the writer was that the Corinthians were short of Christ. They were short of the enjoyment of Christ, short of the eating of Christ. They had to realize that they all had taken Christ as their Passover, not only for redeeming but also for feeding. Following this they kept the feast by taking Christ as the unleavened bread. Do not merely learn the teachings. This will kill you. Rather, keep the feast. We have a feast three hundred sixty-five days a year. Every day we Christians have the feast, and we keep this feast by eating Jesus as the unleavened bread.

EATING JESUS AND DRINKING THE FLOW THAT PROCEEDS OUT OF CHRIST

In 10:3-4 Paul said, "And all ate the same spiritual food, and all drank the same spiritual drink; for they drank of a spiritual rock which followed them, and the rock was Christ." This again refers to the enjoyment of Christ. The people of Israel started their spiritual life, their heavenly journey, on the day they ate the Passover, and in the wilderness they ate manna day by day. This type indicates that day by day we have to eat Jesus and drink the flow that proceeds out of Christ. Do not merely learn teachings, and do not try to acquire many gifts. Simply learn to eat. The local churches have to be the eating, drinking churches. They are not churches of teachings or churches of charismatic gifts. We are the eating, drinking church. Day by day we eat Christ and we drink Jesus.

PARTAKING OF THE LORD'S TABLE

First Corinthians 10:21 speaks of partaking of the Lord's table. We are the partakers of the Lord's table. The partakers are the eaters; we all are the eaters of the Lord's table. The table indicates a feast. We are eaters of the Lord's feast. According to the context of chapter ten, the Lord's table is the fulfillment of the ancient peace offering. Verse 18 says, "Look at Israel according to the flesh. Are not those who eat the sacrifices those who have fellowship with the altar?" The altar refers to the peace offering. In the peace offering there were five portions. There was a portion for God, a portion for the ministering priest, a portion for the offerer, a portion for all the priests, and a portion for all the people who were present. All the people who were there had the privilege to participate in the peace offering in the presence of God, and they took their portion with God. All, including God, were eaters. God was one of the eaters, the priest that ministered was one of the eaters, the offerer was one of the eaters, the priest's family were the eaters, and all the people who were there were the eaters. They all ate the same thing for fellowship, and they had peace with God and peace with one another. Now at the Lord's table when we eat the bread, there is a portion for God, and there is a portion for all of us. We all are enjoying Christ in the presence of God with peace. There is the real peace between us and God, and there is the real peace among ourselves, one with another. This is the participation, the enjoyment, of Christ. This enjoyment of Christ is for the growth.

REMEMBERING THE LORD
BY EATING AND DRINKING HIM

Following chapter ten is the Lord's supper in chapter eleven. Although I was in Christianity for many years, and I attended the so-called communion many times, I never heard anyone say that to remember the Lord is to eat Him and to drink Him. The Lord Jesus told us to eat and drink in remembrance of Him (11:24-25; Matt. 26:26-27). The proper remembrance of the Lord is to eat and drink Him. To have the remembrance of a certain loved one is to exercise our mind to recall the goodness and virtues that person had. But to remember the Lord Jesus is not that way. To remember the Lord Jesus is to eat Him, to take Him in. "Take, eat; this is My body" (Matt. 26:26); "this do unto the remembrance of Me"

(1 Cor. 11:24). "Drink of it, all of you, for this is My blood" (Matt. 26:27-28); "this do, as often as you drink it, unto the remembrance of Me" (1 Cor. 11:25).

The Lord's table is an exhibition of our daily life. Day by day we live by eating Jesus. He said, "He who eats Me, he also shall live because of Me" (John 6:57). Day by day we eat Jesus and we live by Jesus. Then on the first day of the week we come together to make a declaration to the whole universe. We may say, "Satan, angels, demons, all come and see. Our way of living day by day is to eat Jesus. Now we come to the Lord's table for an exhibition. This is our life, and this is our daily walk." However, if we do not have such a life and daily walk, the Lord's table meeting is merely a performance. In this case, the church becomes a theater for actors and actresses to perform something. This is not genuine. This is not an exhibition, a declaration. Rather, it is a performance. The Lord's table meeting should not be a performance. It must be an exhibition, a declaration, made by us to all the beings in the universe. I hope that whenever we have the Lord's table, we would make such a declaration: "Oh, all beings, come and see! Satan, come and see! All the angels, all the demons, and all creatures, come and see! Our way to live is to eat and drink Jesus." Now we exhibit this living to the whole universe. This is the remembrance of the Lord Jesus.

TRANSFORMED BY EATING JESUS

First Corinthians 12:13 says we "were all given to drink one Spirit." The way to drink is in verse 3: "Therefore I make known to you that no one speaking in the Spirit of God says, Jesus is accursed; and no one can say, Jesus is Lord! except in the Holy Spirit." Whenever we say, "Lord Jesus," we are in the spirit. When we say, "O Lord Jesus," we are drinking. This is to take in the living water.

In 3:6 Paul said, "I planted, Apollos watered, but God caused the growth." By drinking we get the watering, and the watering is for growing. Following growth is the transformation. As we have seen, the church is a farm for growing plants, but eventually all the plants are transformed into precious materials—gold, silver, and precious stones (v. 12). This is not an outward change, but a change in life. The Greek word for *transformation* is anglicized as *metamorphosis*. Metamorphosis is a metabolic change. It is not a change by outward improvement but a kind of chemical change. A new element is added into us, nourishing us, discharging all the old things and replacing them with something new. Metamorphosis is a change in life with a new element replacing the old. This is the very meaning of transformation.

The way to have this change is by eating. If our face is pale, we may use cosmetics to change its color. This is an outward change, not a transformation. However, if day by day we take steak, chicken, milk, eggs, and fruit, after two months our face will be shining. This is not a mere outward change but a transformation. Day by day we eat Jesus as the heavenly steak and chicken. By this eating we have growth, and with the growth there is transformation. By transformation we are no more the wood, grass, and stubble; we become gold, silver, and precious stones.

TRANSFORMATION FOR THE BUILDING

In the New Jerusalem there is nothing muddy or wooden. Everything there is gold, pearls, and precious stones. Paul was a marvelous writer. He said, "According to the grace of God given to me, as a wise master builder I have laid a foundation, and another builds upon it. But let each man take heed how he builds upon it....But if anyone builds upon the foundation gold, silver, precious stones, wood, grass, stubble" (3:10, 12). We do not know how he received the concept of gold, silver, and precious stones, but this concept is very scriptural. In a previous chapter we have seen that the two ends of the Bible as well as the sections between the ends speak of gold, silver, and precious stones. These are the precious materials which are good for the building of God's house, God's city, the church.

The church is built only with precious materials. There is no clay, burnt brick, or anything wooden or natural. All the materials have to be transformed. Precious stones are not merely created by God. They are something of God's creation that have passed through a process of being burned and pressed. This is transformation. Today we all are under the process of being transformed. Second Corinthians 3:18 says, "We all with unveiled face, beholding and reflecting like a mirror the glory of the Lord, are being transformed into the same image from glory to glory, even as from the Lord Spirit." Romans 12:2 says that in order to have the Body life we must "be transformed by the renewing of the mind." Many Christians today talk about the Body life according to Romans 12, but they neglect the word *transformed*. Without being transformed there is no possibility for us to have the Body life. The Body life is not something natural; it is not something brought about by our work. The Body life is something of Christ wrought into us. Therefore, we need transformation. Every part of our natural being has to be transformed so that we will be no more "wood" but "petrified wood." This is the concept of 1 Corinthians. May the Lord be merciful to us. We need a deliverance from teachings and gifts into the enjoyment and eating of Christ. Then we will have the growth, transformation, and building.

We must pray not only for ourselves but for others also. We are in the Lord's recovery. The Lord is recovering something, but many seeking ones in today's Christianity are short in their concept. Therefore, pray for them and pray for yourselves that you may receive what is needed. In the Lord's recovery today what is needed is the real enjoyment of Christ. This Christ is the life-giving Spirit (15:45b), and we all have been made, positioned, to drink of this one Spirit, the all-inclusive Christ. The one Spirit is nothing less than Christ Himself as the life-giving Spirit. This is the all-inclusive Christ for us to enjoy. We need this enjoyment.

CHAPTER NINE

CHRIST AS LIFE
FOR THE PREPARATION OF THE BRIDE

Scripture Reading: Gen. 2:18-23; John 3:6b, 29-30; 12:24;
19:34; Matt. 13:3, 24; 1 Cor. 3:6, 9b; Rev. 19:7; 21:2, 9b

In Genesis 2:21-23 Eve was presented to Adam as a bride;
in John 3:29 the believers are a bride to Christ as the Bridegroom; and in the book of Revelation, at the conclusion of
the Bible, the bride is mentioned again (21:2, 9; 22:17). In this
chapter we will see how the bride is prepared.

THE BRIDE IN GENESIS AND REVELATION

The Bible is very consistent in how it begins and how it
ends. It begins and ends with the tree of life (Gen. 2:9; Rev.
2:7; 22:2, 14, 19), and it begins and ends with a flowing river
(Gen. 2:10; Rev. 22:1). It begins with three kinds of precious
materials—gold, bdellium, precious stones—and it ends with
gold, pearl, and precious stones (Gen. 2:11-12; Rev. 21:18-21).
It begins with a garden (Gen. 2:8), and it ends with a city (Rev.
21:2). In this way, the two ends of the Bible mirror one
another.

At the beginning and end of the Bible there is also a bride.
The difference between the two is that the bride in the beginning is only a type, a prefigure, a foreshadowing, of the
coming bride. This may be compared to a person who sends
her photograph before she comes to visit you. Her picture
gives you a general idea of who she is, but when the person
herself comes, you know her more definitely. In the beginning
of the Bible there is a picture of the bride. At the end of the
Bible comes the bride herself, who is now ready.

THE CHURCH BEING THE BRIDE OF CHRIST

In the New Testament the bride is the church, the counterpart of Christ who is the Man in the universe (Eph. 5:25-32). In Genesis 2:18 God said, "It is not good for the man to be alone." This refers to Christ (Rom. 5:14). It is not good for Christ to be alone without the church. Christ needs the church. As a young Christian I was told that there are many mansions in the heavens, waiting to be filled with saved sinners. However, in the Bible there is something much more meaningful than mansions in heaven. It is that the glorious Christ, the universal Man, needs a bride. God said it is not good for Christ to be alone. Christ needs a bride.

THE PREPARATION OF THE BRIDE TYPIFIED IN THE OLD TESTAMENT

In what way does God prepare the bride for Christ? We must look at the type. The types are pictures. Little children in kindergarten like books with pictures. If you tell children about a dog, they may still wonder what a dog is, but if you show them a picture of a dog, immediately they get the idea.

Genesis 2 gives us a picture of how the bride comes into existence. After Adam was created, God looked at him and said, "It is not good for the man to be alone; I will make him a helper as his counterpart" (v. 18). God then brought all the cattle, beasts, and birds before Adam to see what he would name them. When Adam saw the dog, he may have said, "No. This is not my counterpart. This is a dog." When God brought the cat to Adam, he might have looked at himself and said, "I have two legs, but this creature has four legs. This is not my counterpart. This is a cat." In this way he named each of the living creatures. However, Adam did not find anything that matched him. This must have been a disappointment to Adam.

After this, God caused Adam to sleep, opened his side, took a rib, and with the rib built a woman (vv. 21-23). God then brought the woman to Adam. When Adam saw the woman, he seemed to say, "This is my counterpart. I am a man and she is a woman." Adam and Eve were a couple. Eve, the bride, was produced from something coming out of Adam to be his increase. When a young man is single, he has no increase, but when he is married, he has an increase. In the same way, Eve was the increase of Adam. The bride is the increase of the man, the increase of the bridegroom.

THE PREPARATION OF THE BRIDE
FULFILLED IN THE NEW TESTAMENT

Adam was a type of Christ, the Man, and Eve was a type of the church as the bride to Christ (Eph. 5:25-32). In Christianity we heard many messages telling us that we were sinful and that Christ died on the cross for our sins. This is true, but these messages never told us that Christ died on the cross to produce the church. Adam was a type of Christ, and Adam's sleep was a type of the death of Christ on the cross. In God's economy Christ had to die; He had to "sleep." God caused Christ to sleep on the cross.

In one sense, Christ died on the cross for our sins, but in another sense, He slept on the cross. While He was sleeping, His side was pierced and out came blood and water (John 19:34). The blood is for the cleansing of our sins (1:29; Heb. 9:22); the water is for imparting life (John 12:24; 3:14-15). With Eve in Genesis 2 there was no sin, so there was no need of the blood; the rib alone was needed. However, since at the time Jesus died on the cross, man had become involved with sin, there was the need not only for water to impart life but for the blood to cleanse us of our sins.

TWO ASPECTS OF THE DEATH OF CHRIST

The Gospel of John presents these two aspects concerning the death of Christ. Verse 29 of chapter one says, "Behold, the Lamb of God, who takes away the sin of the world!" This is the first aspect of Christ's death, to deal with sins. Then 12:24 says, "Unless the grain of wheat falls into the ground and dies, it abides alone; but if it dies, it bears much fruit." This aspect of the death of Christ has nothing to do with sin. This aspect of His death is for producing many grains to form one loaf. This loaf is the church (1 Cor. 10:17).

The church was produced by the life-imparting water. What is this water? First Corinthians 10:4 indicates that this water is the Spirit. Christ is typified by the rock which was cleft, out of which came living water. That living water signifies the life-giving Spirit (1 Cor. 15:45b). When Jesus died on the cross, He was cleft, and the life-water, the life-giving Spirit, issued forth.

By what means is the church produced? The church is produced by the life-giving Spirit. John 3:6 says, "That which is born of the Spirit is spirit." The same chapter also says, "He who has the bride is the bridegroom....He must increase, but I must decrease" (vv. 29-30). Few Christians realize that regeneration is not only for our salvation but also for the producing of the church. Regeneration is not only for us to be born again. It is also for the purpose of producing the bride.

THE CHURCH BEING THE INCREASE OF CHRIST

The church is not Americans, British, Germans, Japanese, Chinese, and Puerto Ricans coming together. The church is the increase of Christ. That the church is the increase of Christ means that the church is Christ. Colossians 3:10-11 says, "And have put on the new man, which is being renewed unto full knowledge according to the image of Him who created him, where there cannot be Greek and Jew, circumcision and uncircumcision, barbarian, Scythian, slave, free man, but Christ is all and in all." In the new man, which is the church, Christ is all and in all. Therefore, the church is the increase of Christ. In the church there is no black or white; there is only Christ as all in all.

The church is the increase of Christ; therefore, it is a part of Christ. Only the life-giving Spirit with the life of Christ can make people a part of Christ to produce His counterpart, His increase. This is not a matter of teachings or gifts. It is absolutely a matter of life. No teaching or gift of any kind can produce the increase of Christ. I am not against any proper doctrine, nor am I against any genuine gift. All the proper doctrines and every genuine gift have their place. For the producing of the church, however, our unique need is the growth in life.

Ephesians, a book on the church, does not say anything about teachings or gifts for the producing of the church.

Instead, Ephesians says that we all have to grow into Christ the Head in all things (4:15). In this sense, the book of Ephesians helps us to be delivered from teachings (v. 14). For the church to be the increase of Christ, we do not need the knowledge collected from teachings or the manifested gifts. We need growth.

GROWTH IN LIFE REVEALED IN MATTHEW 13

The growth in life is revealed in Matthew 13. In this chapter the Lord Jesus told us that He came not as a teacher but as a Sower to sow Himself as the seed of life into us (vv. 3-8). This is very meaningful. We must drop the concept that we can be wonderful, spiritual Christians by collecting knowledge. We must be revolutionized in our concept. The Lord came as a Sower, and He sowed Himself into us as the seed of life. According to Matthew 13, after this sowing, we all need to grow.

The first parable in Matthew 13 reveals the sower (vv. 3-8). In the second parable the seed sown grows up into wheat (vv. 24-30). Then the fourth parable refers to fine flour (vv. 33-35). Fine flour comes from the grains of wheat. These grains are good for making a loaf, and this loaf signifies the Body of Christ (1 Cor. 10:17). We are many members yet one Body, one bread.

In the fifth and sixth parables a treasure is hidden in a field, and a merchant finds a pearl of great value (vv. 44-46). In principle, the treasure hidden in the field must be composed of gold and precious stones, items which are transformed substances. These transformed items are the materials for building the house of God (1 Cor. 3:12). This is very meaningful. For the producing of the church we need growth and transformation. Then we can have the building. The growth is for transformation, and transformation is for building.

GROWTH IN LIFE BY FEEDING, NOT BY TEACHINGS

Many in Christianity hold the wrong concept that teachings are needed for growth in life. Christianity cares too much for teachings. Satan is very subtle. In fundamental Christianity he has used dead teachings to cover people's eyes. Teachings upon teachings are like layers upon layers covering people's eyes. The more they study theology, commentaries, and expositions, the more they are blinded, covered, and veiled. More than thirty years ago I had many layers of veils over my eyes. It took more than fifteen years for all the veils to be removed. To grow in life we need feeding. Regardless of how much we teach others to grow, no growth will take place. Teaching does not help the growth, but feeding does. We must help the brothers and sisters to eat and drink.

Ephesians 4:14 says, "Tossed by waves and carried about by every wind of teaching." It does not say by the "wind of heresy" but by the "wind of teaching." This teaching is not false doctrine but good, sound, scriptural, and fundamental doctrine. It is doctrine as wind that carries people away from the Body, from the church, and from the Head, Christ. In the Lord's recovery He has released us and freed us to come back to Himself and to His Body. Now in the church I am so happy. Forty years ago I was distracted by knowledge, but praise the Lord, now I am liberated and recovered! I do not care for mere doctrine. I only care for Christ and the church, for the Head and the Body.

THE GIFTS NOT HELPING US TO GROW IN LIFE

The exercise of the gifts does not help our growth in life. Some people consider that we need gifts such as divine healing, but for a person to receive divine healing will not help him to grow in life. Some using 1 Corinthians 14:4 say that tongue-speaking edifies people. However, if we check into the tongue-speaking practiced today, much of it is not genuine. Some people lay hands on others, telling them to say, "Praise Jesus," quickly over and over, or to speak nonsensical syllables. To be honest, this kind of speaking in tongues does not help people to grow.

Genuine Tongues Being a Dialect

Pentecostal Christianity, reacting to the deadness of fundamental Christianity, cares mainly for the gifts, especially tongue-speaking. I spoke in tongues more than thirty-five years ago, but after carefully studying the Bible concerning this matter, I dropped this practice. By looking into the Bible with a Greek-English interlinear text, I discovered that the word *tongue* is two words in Greek. It is either *glossa,* referring to the speaking organ or a dialect, or *dialektos,* meaning "dialect." *Tongues* and *dialect* are used interchangeably in Acts 2:4, 6, 8, and 11. However, some people speak in tongues by uttering nonsensical syllables or by repeating the same syllables over and over. Since they realize that these sounds are not a real dialect, they say that the tongue they are speaking is an unknown dialect or an angelic dialect. However, even the most simple dialect is composed of more than a few sounds.

In 1936 I became very involved with tongue-speaking, but as a student of the Bible I could not get through in my understanding of this matter. At that time I spoke with a certain leading one in the Assembly of God, who came to China from the west coast of the United States. He was over sixty years old and was supposed to be a scholar in Greek and in knowing the Bible. In our conversation, he told me that *glossa* does not necessarily mean a dialect. I then opened to Acts 2 and showed him that *tongues* and *dialect* are used interchangeably. I asked him to reconcile his teaching for me, but he could not. Eventually, he put his hands on my head and said, "Your head is too big." With that he ended our conversation. That was also the end of my tongue-speaking.

In 1963 a new movement of tongue-speaking was very prevailing along the west coast of the United States under the leadership of a certain Episcopalian priest. This movement published a paper in Los Angeles called *Trinity.* In an editorial on the first page of one issue, the writer said that he had contacted two hundred tongue-speakers. Without exception, all two hundred doubted that their speaking in tongues was genuine. Still, because the writer was one hundred percent for tongue-speaking, he encouraged everyone to speak in tongues and not to doubt. Do you believe that Peter and the others doubted their experience of speaking in tongues on the day of Pentecost?

We must see through the subtlety of the enemy. If we ask a linguist to analyze a recording of man-made speaking in tongues, he will verify that it is false. Moreover, after someone speaks in tongues, someone else may interpret it, saying, "My people, time is short; I am coming quickly." However, in the evening the same tongue may be spoken and interpreted as, "Be on the alert; there will be an earthquake." The children of God should not be so foolish.

In 1963 I was invited to San Diego by a group of people who spoke in tongues. While I was there, one of the leaders turned to another Chinese brother and me and said, "Praise the Lord, God has given me the grace to speak Chinese!" He tried to speak something in Chinese, and then he turned to me to see whether or not I understood it. I said, "Brother, I'm sorry. I did not understand one word you spoke." Then he began to speak again, uttering some sounds in a different way. Again, he turned to me, and I said, "I still do not understand anything." He tried a third time, but the other brother and I still could not understand what he uttered. I told him, "I speak Mandarin and this brother speaks Cantonese. Between the two of us, we know the main dialects of Chinese. We cannot speak many of them, but we still can recognize them. However, we cannot understand one word of your speaking." His was a man-made tongue.

Later, in one of the meetings of that congregation, an American woman in her fifties stood up and spoke a short sentence in a so-called tongue. Then a young American-born Chinese of about twenty years of age stood and interpreted her short tongue-speaking with a long interpretation. After the meeting, as a guest in the leader's home, I asked him if he thought that the interpretation by the young Chinese man was genuine. He said, "No, I do not believe that it was genuine." Two years later in Waco, Texas I met the young Chinese man who did the interpretation in San Diego. When I asked him about his interpretation of the tongue-speaking, he admitted that it was not a real interpretation. I can tell you many stories like this. I am not speaking something that I do not know. I have passed through these things, and I realize the real situation.

I do believe that there are genuine tongues today, but many so-called tongues spoken today are only human-manufactured tongues. In 1964 I was invited to dinner at the home of a brother who held a doctorate in physics. He shared with me his testimony about how he began to speak in tongues. He said that he spoke in tongues by exercising his jaw and turning his tongue a certain way. Then I responded by saying, "Brother, do you believe that on the day of Pentecost Peter turned his jaw a certain way?" After listening to his testimony, I realized that under the Lord's mercy what I had experienced was much better than this. Because this brother was trained in a certain way by his denomination, he exercised his jaw and turned his tongue to make a strange sound which he call a tongue. However, there is no need to do this. Without doing this we can enjoy the Lord's grace much more than he did.

"Do All Speak in Tongues?"

In this century, perhaps no one has been used by the Lord as much as Watchman Nee. I was his co-worker for twenty years. When I was speaking in tongues in 1936 in North China, he sent me a cable, saying, "Not all speak in tongues." He had the position to send such a cable to me because he was senior to me, and I was his junior. He advised me to be careful concerning tongue-speaking. Brother Nee never spoke in tongues. Some have said that speaking in tongues is the unique manifestation of the gifts, but he strongly disagreed with this. Many spiritual giants never spoke in tongues. We should not be fooled. Some fundamental teachers, however, following the teaching of J. N. Darby, say that speaking in tongues and other manifestations of the gifts are dispensationally over. We do not agree with this; it is too extreme. We cannot say that the gifts are over. They are still here, but they need to be genuine.

THE PRIMARY NEED IN THE LORD'S RECOVERY

At certain times in the Lord's recovery, and according to the need, the Lord has given us knowledge and teaching, and He also has given us certain gifts. In the past, we have had healings, but the Lord has made it very clear to us that the primary need in His recovery is not teachings or gifts but life. Life is Christ Himself as the all-inclusive Spirit. In the Lord's recovery, we need the growth in life. Therefore, if you speak in tongues, I do not oppose you and I do not want to bother you; however, I advise you not to become addicted to it.

If we read and pray-read the New Testament again and again, we will see that our primary need is Jesus Christ, who became the life-giving Spirit as our life and life supply. At a certain point, for a certain need, the Lord may allow us to have certain teachings, and He may also allow us to have certain gifts as a kind of help. These, however, are not the normal things. The normal Christian life is a life of living by Christ. "He who eats Me, he also shall live because of Me" (John 6:57b). It is by this that the members of Christ are produced; it is by this that the Body of Christ is built up; and it is by this that the bride will be prepared for the Bridegroom.

LIFE, NOT GIFTS AND TEACHINGS, IN THE WRITINGS OF JOHN

In Genesis the bride is mentioned in type. In the Gospel of John and the book of Revelation, however, the bride is mentioned in fulfillment. In his writings, John never touched anything of the gifts or of mere teachings. John had a ministry of life. He wrote, "That which is born of the Spirit is spirit"; this refers to regeneration, which is for the increase of Christ to prepare the bride for the Bridegroom (John 3:6, 29). John also tells us that Christ is the unique grain of wheat who fell into the earth, died, and produced many grains (12:24). We are these many grains. We are the reproduction, continuation, spread, growth, and increase of Christ not by teachings or gifts, but by Christ Himself as the life and life supply.

In the book of Revelation we do not find mere teachings or gifts; rather, we find life. Revelation 2:7 says, "To him who overcomes, to him I will give to eat of the tree of life," and 2:17 says, "To him who overcomes, to him I will give of the hidden manna." Then 3:20 says, "If anyone hears My voice and opens the door, then I will come in to him and dine with him and he with Me." Moreover, there are no teachings or gifts in the New Jerusalem. There is only the flow of the living water, and on either side of the river of life grows the tree of life, producing twelve fruits (22:1-2). The river and the tree become the full supply to the entire city. This is the clear picture in the Bible.

We all have to be preserved in the proper realization of the church life. The Lord's recovery of the church life is absolutely by Himself as our life and life supply. We must never be distracted by any teaching or gift from Christ as our life and life supply. It is by Him as our life and life supply that we can be the members of His Body, and it is by Him as our life and life supply that the bride can be prepared for His coming back. May the Lord be merciful to us. I pray that we all will see a clear vision and not merely have an understanding of certain teachings or doctrines. The church as the Body of Christ is the increase of Christ. We have to take Him, we have to eat Him, and we have to live by Him. Then we will be prepared as the bride for His coming back.

CHAPTER TEN

LIFE, GROWTH, AND TRANSFORMATION FOR THE BUILDING

Scripture Reading: 2 Cor. 3:6, 17-18; 1:8-9; 4:7-8, 10; 12:9; Rom. 8:28-29

Transformation is a matter of life. However, we must realize that transformation is not simple. Because there are certain negative factors with us, life alone cannot work out an adequate transformation. We need something further. First Corinthians brings us to transformation, but it does not say much about the way to be transformed. The word *transformed* is used in 2 Corinthians chapter three. Verse 6 of chapter three says, "Who has also made us sufficient as ministers of a new covenant, ministers not of the letter but of the Spirit; for the letter kills, but the Spirit gives life." This confirms that teachings do not work. The word *letter* refers to teachings and doctrines in letter. All the teachings and doctrines do a killing work. The letter kills, but the Spirit gives life. Verse 17 says, "And the Lord is the Spirit; and where the Spirit of the Lord is, there is freedom." The Spirit in verse 17 is the Spirit who gives life. Verse 18 continues: "But we all with unveiled face, beholding and reflecting like a mirror the glory of the Lord, are being transformed into the same image from glory to glory, even as from the Lord Spirit." In these verses transformation is related to the Spirit who is life. The Spirit is the very life, and life is the transforming factor. It is this life that transforms us into the image of the Lord.

TRANSFORMATION BY "COOKING"

After chapter three, however, chapter four is necessary because for transformation the Spirit alone is not adequate.

For good cooking you need water in a cooking vessel, but water alone is not adequate. Good cooking requires two opposing elements. There must be water within and fire without. We need water in the pot, and we need fire under the pot. Cooking is a kind of transformation. Raw fish does not taste very good. We must cook the fish, and by cooking it we transform it from one taste to another taste. After being cooked, the fish becomes very delicious. It has been transformed by cooking.

Cooking requires water within and fire without. The Spirit is the real water. We all have the "water" within, but we also need the fire. If we only had chapter three of 2 Corinthians we may say, "Transformation is wonderful and marvelous. It is by the life-giving Spirit. And the Lord is the Spirit!" In our hymnal we have songs about the Spirit, but we need more songs about "burning," "baking," and "cooking." We need to be put into the "oven," and we need to stay there for a period of time. For the sisters, their dear husband is the best oven. Sometimes one oven is not good enough. The sisters also need some little ovens. After two or three years of marriage without children, many women are desirous to have a child. This is wonderful, but they must be warned: All the little ones are little "ovens."

Verse 7 of chapter four says, "But we have this treasure in earthen vessels." We are just earthen vessels, but we have a treasure within. However, verse 8 continues, "We are pressed on every side." For the sake of the pressing, we need "helpers" on every side. I do agree that many young ones among us need to be married, and I would encourage them to marry. They should not marry too young, but sooner or later the Lord will put them into the oven. Just as a normal family always has an oven, the family itself is an "oven." Do not try to escape from the oven. To prepare to get married is to get ready to be put into the oven. I never speak flowery words about marriage. To speak in this way is to cheat you. In a sense marriage is wonderful, but in another sense it is awful. Those who are married have experienced this. A wife is a good oven and also a good dessert. If you are going to enjoy the dessert, you must be prepared to suffer the oven.

Even in the church life there are some "ovens." As we have seen, by pray-reading and by the life-giving Spirit we all are one. However, the oven is still among us. Sometimes the brothers are the oven to the sisters, and sometimes the sisters are an oven to the brothers.

BEING PRESSED TO TRUST IN THE GOD
WHO RAISES THE DEAD

Paul also said they were "unable to find a way out" (v. 8b). He did not know what to do or what to say. Verse 10 says, "Always bearing about in the body the putting to death of Jesus." In 1:8 and 9 Paul said, "For we do not want you to be ignorant, brothers, of our affliction which befell us in Asia, that we were excessively burdened, beyond our power, so that we despaired even of living. Indeed we ourselves had the response of death in ourselves, that we should not base our confidence on ourselves but on God, who raises the dead." They had the sentence of death; they had the sensation that they were going to die. They were pressed to such an extent that they despaired of living, so they learned not to trust in themselves. They were pressed out of themselves. They were pressed to give up their trust in themselves. They were pressed to trust in God, the God of resurrection, the God who raises the dead.

We may say, "I do not trust in myself. I trust in the Lord." To say this is easy. We do not know how much we cheat ourselves in saying this. It is not easy to lose our trust in ourselves. Every one among us is a self-trusting one. It is really hard for us to get rid of self-trust. Even little children have self-trust. They may love their mother very much, but they do not trust in their mother; they trust in themselves. The more a child grows, the more that child trusts in himself. A mother realizes that after a child becomes five years of age he no longer trusts in her. The more one grows, the more he trusts in himself. For every full-grown man there is the full-grown trust in the self. We may have no trust in others and no trust in the Lord. Our trust is only in ourselves. To learn the lesson not to trust in ourselves but in the Lord is not easy because of our cleverness, wisdom, natural strength, and natural motive. We need many years to be rid of our natural cleverness, natural wisdom, natural strength, and natural motive.

In cooking certain foods, fifteen minutes in the oven may be good enough, but sometimes we need three hours, and sometimes we need a whole day. I have been put into the "oven" for over forty-five years. Today I am still in the oven. Regardless of how nice and dear we may be, we are still "raw." We need God's cooking. We are pressed on every side; we are unable to find a way out; we are put to death. Paul said that he bore about in the body the putting to death of Jesus (4:10). This means that when he was on the earth working for the Lord, ministering something to the Lord's children, he was always being put to death. All the time he bore in his mortal body the putting to death. Paul did not have an easy time. If we see this, we may say, "Then I will never be a Christian." But this is not up to us. This is our destiny. It is not our choice; it is God's choice. God's choice is our destiny, and God has predestinated us to be Christians. Even if we try to run away, we cannot give up the Christian faith. Some say it is not easy to stand in the faith, but for Christians it is easier to stand than to fall. We all have been chosen and predestinated to be put into the oven. We cannot run away. It is not up to us; it is not our choice. This is the Lord's choice, and His choice is our destiny.

GOD'S PREDESTINATION FOR US

Recently some young people asked me to fellowship with them about marriage. I told them that thirty-five years ago I had many things to say about marriage. I could give thirty-six points on marriage, but I eventually found out that I was cheated and I was cheating others. Not one of the points worked. Today I have nothing to say about marriage. I do not know who is the best wife or husband for anyone. For over forty years in the church life I have seen all kind of marriages. Now I am perplexed. I do not know who is a good wife or a good husband for someone. Thirty years ago in the Far East there was the custom, especially among the older ones, of recommending a young sister to a young brother or a young brother to a young sister. When we were concerned for a young brother, we recommended a sister to him because we thought she was the best one for him. Sometimes, however, a brother would not take our recommendation. Rather, he would be interested in a sister whom we considered to be peculiar. He chose such a sister to be his wife, but actually it was not his choice; it was God's choice. That peculiar sister was predestinated by God for him.

Sometimes love blinds people. Although we may warn a brother about a sister's peculiarities, he still may consider that he can bear them out of love for her. We may warn him not to have so much trust in himself, that he will be unable to bear such a one and will probably suffer. Such a brother may still marry the peculiar sister, but after only three days he may come back for fellowship with tears on his face. He may say that he prefers to have the windows of his house shut, but she insists to have them open, and he does not know what to do. However, it is too late for fellowship. This sister is his choice and God's destiny for him. He must take God's choice for him. He must go, joyfully suffer, and die. The Lord's grace is sufficient. He cannot bear it, but the grace can.

I have seen many such cases. Certain brothers reject all the better choices and take a peculiar one for their wife. Praise the Lord, that is the right one for them. Such a choice is not an accident. The Lord predestinated such a sister for them before the foundation of the earth. This is why today I have nothing to say about marriage. If you feel that you must be married, go and do it. I do not know who is the best one for you, but the Lord knows. We, the older ones who cared for the younger ones, all became disappointed, so we took our hands off their situation. We are not the good matchmakers. Only the Lord knows who is a match.

No one should ever complain. We must not blame our husband or our wife. We must not blame the situation or condition of our family. Everything is of the Lord, and He knows everything. Even if we make a mistake about marriage, that mistake is right. Actually, there are no mistakes. We must not regret anything. We have to say, "Hallelujah, I made such a mistake, and I need such a mistake. Every mistake is wonderful." Some may say that I am now encouraging mistakes. However, if we make a mistake, it is because the Lord allows us to make that mistake. The Lord Jesus said that even the hairs of our head are all numbered (Matt. 10:30). If He has numbered our hairs, then there is nothing about us that is not under His care. We must never say we married the wrong wife. We can never have the wrong wife. Whosoever we marry is the right one. That one is exactly the one who we need. The Lord knows.

We all have been predestinated by Him. The things that have happened to us are beyond our dreams. Many of us never dreamed that we would be where we are today. This is not of us. We may make a decision about what we will do next year, but only the Lord knows where we will be.

We are in the oven. We may expect that the brothers coordinating with us will be nice, humble, not too slow nor too quick, just fitting our situation. However, they may be just the opposite, and we will suffer. As long as we feel that we are suffering, however, we are wrong. The day we have no feeling of suffering will be the time we are thoroughly cooked. If we still blame our wife or our coordinating brothers, this is proof that we need more cooking. When we are thoroughly cooked, we will have no blame. We will say, "Praise the Lord, the slow one is just as good as the quick one, and the quick one is just as good as the slow one. No one is good, and no one is not good. Everyone is exactly right." This may prove that we have been thoroughly cooked.

Young men and young women, on the one hand, your eyes must be open. However, there is not one woman on this earth who can be the best wife, and there is not one man on this earth who can be the best husband. If we are clear to such an extent, we can then shut our eyes and leave the matter of marriage to the hand of the Lord. We are in His hand. The Lord really knows.

Paul says, "Our outer man is decaying" (2 Cor. 4:16). To decay, to be consumed, means to be exhausted, to be cut bit by bit, little by little. Our outer man needs to be consumed for our inner man to be renewed. Praise the Lord, we all need marriage. This matter is sovereign of the Lord. If we did not need marriage, many would give it up because it is truly a suffering. A certain proverb says that a dumb person, after eating something bitter, suffers silently. Everyone who marries is so; they must suffer without uttering anything. This is the consuming. The outer man is consumed, but the inner man is being renewed day by day.

REALIZING THE SUFFICIENT GRACE OF THE LORD

We must not forget, however, that without water in the pot the fire will burn the food. We need the fire and we need the water. While our dear wife is cooking us, we must call, "O Lord Jesus." Then the water comes in. This is the way we realize the sufficient grace of the Lord. We should now realize that teaching cannot help us. Teaching can do nothing for us. Paul performed many miracles, but he had a thorn in his flesh (12:7-8). Bible students agree that the thorn must have been a physical disease or ailment. Surely this was not merely a cold or the flu. This must have been something very painful to his physical body. He prayed definitely three times, asking the Lord to take out the thorn, but there was no miracle. It was as if the Lord said, "Do not pray in this way. I will not answer such a prayer. I will allow the thorn to prick you, to put you down, that you may experience My grace and My power." This is the working of grace and power into us through sufferings, not by teaching or by the gifts, but by the experience of transformation, the spiritual cooking.

The grace of the Lord is the Lord Himself, and the power of the Lord is the Lord Himself. "My grace is sufficient for you" means that the Lord is sufficient for you. We have to take Him, and He has to work Himself into us. The working of the Lord's grace can never be accomplished by mere teachings or gifts. It must be by the cooking. When some of the experienced saints speak about the Lord's grace and power, we have the realization that they have something real and weighty. But when some younger ones speak the same thing, using the same words, we do not sense anything real because with them there has not been the sufficient cooking or working of grace.

GROWTH BY LIFE AND TRANSFORMATION

We must not think that the Lord's recovery is a mere revival. The Lord's recovery is the Lord's doing to bring us back to the beginning—to life and the transformation of life. It is by this life with transformation by life that the Lord can have a proper church life for the preparation of His bride. There is no other way. Every revival is something that comes and goes. I have seen many revivals come and go. Some lasted for up to two years, while others lasted less than half a year. In this country it is easy to see various movements, and some reports of them appear in the newspapers and magazines. However, after not too long they are gone. Revivals come and go.

The church life, on the other hand, is an orchard. In an orchard there is planting, fertilizing, watering, caring, and growing. Day by day the trees in an orchard appear the same, but after a few years the trees are grown up, and after another few years they all bear fruit. This is not a revival. This is growth. The church life in the Lord's recovery is exactly like this. We cannot expect that a church in a locality will be built up overnight. If it is, it must be artificial. Artificial flowers may be mass produced overnight, but genuine flowers do not grow in this way. Growth is always steady but slow. We all have to be encouraged to go on, but we should not expect that the church life will grow quickly. However, we will see results in the long run. All the movements will come and go like the sun rising and setting, but the church will still be here. After a few years, if the Lord delays, we will see the church life grow. This growth is by life and by transformation.

Many people today talk much about 1 Corinthians 12, but they rarely speak of 2 Corinthians. It is as if they do not have 2 Corinthians in their Bible. They may even be afraid of 2 Corinthians. However, for the Lord's recovery, we need 2 Corinthians more than 1 Corinthians. In this book there are no more gifts and no more mere teachings. Rather, there are suffering, troubling, perplexing, putting to death, and consuming, and there are no miraculous answers to prayer. It is by all these means that the church life is being built.

I look to the Lord that we all could see these matters and

where we are in the Lord's recovery. We need life, we need growth, and we need transformation. Growth comes from life, and transformation comes from growth plus suffering. So we need the water inside, and we need the fire outside. By this we will have the adequate building up of the church.

ALL THINGS WORKING TOGETHER
FOR OUR CONFORMATION TO THE IMAGE OF CHRIST

Romans 8:28-29 says, "And we know that all things work together for good to those who love God, to those who are called according to His purpose. Because those whom He foreknew, He also predestinated to be conformed to the image of His Son, that He might be the Firstborn among many brothers." If we put these two verses together, we can see that all things work together for good that we might be conformed to the image of Christ. In Romans 8 there is firstly the Spirit, the "water," and then there are the "all things." *All things* in Greek means not only all things but all persons, all entities. All things, persons, and entities work together for good. This is a fact; this is the environment. The Spirit within is the water, and the environment with all things is the fire. Many Christians pay attention to the Spirit in Romans 8, but they do not pay attention to the "all things," and they do not understand that all things work together for our good that we may be conformed to the image of Christ.

First Corinthians 10:13 says, "No temptation has taken you except that which is common to man; and God is faithful, who will not allow that you be tempted beyond what you are able, but will, with the temptation, also make the way out, that you may be able to endure it." This is a consolation. God knows how much we can suffer. Sisters who cook know how high the heat should be. If the heat is too high, the food will burn. God also makes the way out. The way out is up to Him. Do not try to escape by yourself. God allows temptation, and God also makes the way out that we may be able to endure it. In this regard 2 Corinthians 12:9 says, "My grace is sufficient for you." The Lord is sovereign. We are the "Jacobs." We can supplant and struggle, but the Lord will still give us an

"Esau" and a "Laban" (Gen. 27:41; 31:36-41). This is for our transformation and conformation to the image of Christ.

CHAPTER ELEVEN

MINISTERING CHRIST BY PROPHESYING

Scripture Reading: 1 Cor. 1:7a; 12:1-13, 27-31; 13:1-2, 8, 11; 14:1, 4-6, 12, 18-19, 23-26, 31-32, 39

TEACHINGS AND GIFTS BEING RELATED TO CHILDREN

Ephesians 4 mentions the teachings of doctrines, while 1 Corinthians 12 and 14 speak about the gifts. Ephesians 4:13-14 says, "Until we all arrive at the oneness of the faith and of the full knowledge of the Son of God, at a full-grown man, at the measure of the stature of the fullness of Christ, that we may be no longer little children tossed by waves and carried about by every wind of teaching in the slight of men, in craftiness with a view to a system of error." These verses indicate that the teachings of doctrines are related to little children.

First Corinthians 13:8 says, "Love never falls away. But whether prophecies, they will be rendered useless; or tongues, they will cease; or knowledge, it will be rendered useless." Prophecies, tongues, and knowledge are gifts, as mentioned in 12:8-10. In 13:11 Paul says, "When I was a child, I spoke as a child, I thought as a child, I reasoned as a child; since I have become a man, I have done away with childish things." By the context of these verses we can see that the gifts are also childish things. Christianity today pays full attention to these two categories of things, the teachings and the gifts. The fundamentalists are for the teachings, and the Pentecostals are for the gifts, but they do not see that these two categories of things are related to children.

The Ephesians were children in doctrines, and the Corinthians were children in the gifts. Are we still children in doctrines and the gifts? Today's Christianity is thickly clouded with teachings and gifts. There is no clear sky there. Many there put their trust either in their gifts or teachings, but we have to see that in the New Testament both teachings and gifts are childish things. This is the clear teaching of the Bible.

CARRIED ABOUT BY EVERY WIND OF TEACHING

If we still take the way of teaching, we are children, tossed by waves and carried about by every wind of teaching. We may illustrate the winds of teaching by a young brother who has recently been saved and is in the church. Today he appreciates the church very much, but when he visits a certain place, some may come to him to teach him. They may ask, "What kind of church do you go to?" If the brother answers, "It is an eating and drinking church," they may say, "This is nonsense. In John 13 the Lord Jesus tells us that we all have to wash one another's feet to show love one to another. Does the church you go to practice foot-washing? The Lord charges us to follow His pattern. Why does the church you go to not practice this? That is wrong. We have a little group here in a home, and every Sunday we have the Lord's table. Before taking the table we all wash one another's feet." The young brother may be convinced by this talk, and he may join this foot-washing group and forget about the church. This is to be carried about by the wind of the teaching of foot-washing. Others may be carried away by some other teaching.

If people ask us whether the church practices this kind of foot-washing, we cannot say no because in the local churches we do not make anything legal or formal. We cannot say that we do not have foot-washing. I myself have washed others' feet in this way, and others have washed my feet. However, this is not the main concern of the church. The main matter is our faith in Christ and the Body of Christ. In these days I look to the Lord that we will spend time to see the unique faith. We have to keep the faith, and we have to be the Body. We should not be carried about by any wind of doctrine.

If there is the possibility that we will be carried about by the wind of doctrine, this proves that we are still childish. All little children love toys, but no grandfather or grandmother still likes toys. The younger we are, the more we love toys. As we grow, we drop all the toys. Teachings are good things but childish. Likewise, gifts are good but childish. This is not merely my word. Paul clearly points out that if we are childish, we will be carried away by the teachings, and we will "play" with the gifts.

THE PROBLEM OF HUMAN-MANUFACTURED SPEAKING IN TONGUES

I wish to impress you that in the New Testament, teachings and gifts are childish. We cannot say that teachings and gifts are wrong if they are genuine, but some teachings and gifts are not genuine. *Tongues* in the New Testament means a dialect. How can any strange sound made with the tongue be a dialect? Some may say that this strange speaking is the dialect of angels, but how can angels speak in such a way? Those who say this are deceiving themselves. These are not the genuine tongues; these are the human-manufactured tongues. Some exhort others to turn their tongue, exercise their jaw, and utter anything but English. On the day of Pentecost, no one asked Peter to turn his tongue, exercise his jaw, and utter anything but his own language. Tongues-speaking is something miraculous, something supernatural. As a supernatural thing, there is no need for anyone to teach others how to do it. Many times I told those who practice this that the case of Balaam and his donkey in the Old Testament is a case of the genuine speaking in tongues (Num. 22:28-30). It was miraculous and supernatural. All of a sudden a donkey spoke a human language. Balaam did not tell his donkey to turn his tongue and exercise his jaw.

People in the tongues-speaking movement first give a lecture to people and some testimonies to inspire them. Then they ask, "Are you interested in speaking in tongues? Come into this room with us." Five or ten people may come into the room with you, and one will exhort you to say, "Praise Jesus! Praise Jesus!", the faster the better. They may then lay hands on your head and tell you to turn your tongue, exercise your jaw, and speak anything but your mother tongue. In San

Diego in 1963, I and a few others stayed in the same home as guests. The host was clear that I was strongly against the false speaking in tongues. After one night's meeting when I had gone to bed, he and his wife tried to help one of the Chinese-speaking brothers to speak in tongues. The host laid hands on him and told him to speak anything except Chinese and English. Because this went on for a long time, a second brother, speaking in Chinese, told the first brother to speak anything, even nonsense. Because the first brother's wife was a Chinese woman born in Indonesia, he had learned something of the Indonesian language, so he spoke some nonsense in that language. The host and his wife were excited and began to applaud. The next morning the brothers told me the whole story. I recounted it to the host and asked him, "Brother, is Christ not good enough for us to preach? Why did you have to do this?" In the so-called Charismatic movement there are many stories like this. I was there and I saw this. This is why I am so strong in this matter. I am not against anything that is genuine. I believe that today the genuine tongues-speaking is still on the earth. God is living, and He is still miraculous and supernatural. However, I cannot believe in the false, human-manufactured tongues.

EVEN GENUINE GIFTS BEING CHILDISH

Even the genuine tongues are still something childish. First Corinthians 13:8 and 11 say, "Love never falls away. But whether prophecies, they will be rendered useless; or tongues, they will cease; or knowledge, it will be rendered useless....When I was a child, I spoke as a child, I thought as a child, I reasoned as a child; since I have become a man, I have done away with childish things." If we read the context of these verses, we must admit that the childish things are the gifts. Even the genuine gifts, the real gifts, are childish things.

THE MANIFESTATION OF THE SPIRIT

In Christianity today the traditional teaching about gifts is not trustworthy. One traditional teaching concerning the meetings says that there are nine gifts as manifestations of the Spirit. However, 1 Corinthians 12:7 does not use the word *manifestations* in the plural. It uses *manifestation* in the singular. Verses 7 to 10 say, "But to each one is given the manifestation of the Spirit for what is profitable. For to one through the Spirit a word of wisdom is given, and to another a word of knowledge, according to the same Spirit; to a different one faith in the same Spirit, and to another gifts of healing in the one Spirit, and to another operations of works of power, and to another prophecy, and to another discerning of spirits; to a different one various kinds of tongues, and to another interpretation of tongues." In these verses Paul mentioned nine items in the list of the gifts, but do you believe the manifestation of the Spirit is only in these nine items? Verse 28 of the same chapter says, "And God has placed some in the church: first apostles, second prophets, third teachers; then works of power, then gifts of healing, helps, administrations, various kinds tongues." In the list in verses 7 through 10 nothing is mentioned concerning helps and administrations. Acts 2:17 also says, "And it shall be in the last days, says God, that I will pour out of My Spirit upon all flesh, and your sons and your daughters shall prophesy, and your young men shall see visions, and your old men shall dream things in dreams." Visions and dreams are also the manifestation of the Spirit, but these two items are not mentioned in 1 Corinthians 12. In 1 Corinthians 12:7-10 Paul lists only certain items of the manifestation of the Spirit as illustrations. This list does not include all the items. There are many items of the manifestation of the Spirit.

In the same way, the traditional teaching in Christianity tells people that the fruit of the Spirit is only nine items. Galatians 5:22-23a says, "But the fruit of the Spirit is love, joy, peace, long-suffering, kindness, goodness, faithfulness, meekness, self-control." Do you believe that the fruit of the Spirit is only these nine items? What about humility, righteousness, and holiness? These virtues are not mentioned in Galatians 5. Many other kinds of spiritual virtues are also not mentioned, but every kind of spiritual virtue is a fruit of the Spirit. The apostle Paul listed only some as an illustration. The fruit of the Holy Spirit is not only of nine kinds. Similarly, the manifestation of the Spirit is not only of nine items. Only nine items are mentioned as an illustration. At least four items are clearly mentioned in the Bible as the manifestation of the Spirit but are not listed in 1 Corinthians 12—helps, administrations, visions, and dreams. We should not have confidence in the traditional teachings we received from Christianity. They are not trustworthy or adequate. We have to come back to the pure Word.

THE WORD OF WISDOM
AND THE WORD OF KNOWLEDGE

In the list in 1 Corinthians 12, the word of wisdom is first, and the word of knowledge is second (v. 8). These two kinds of words are the first gifts. Tongues and the interpretation of tongues are the last (v. 10). However, the Charismatic movement has made tongues and interpretation the first and nearly the unique gifts. Sometimes certain ones ask us if we have the manifestation of the Spirit in our meetings. I am afraid that some of us would not dare to answer this question. If such a one would ask me if we have the manifestation of the Spirit, I would say that we have it more than others do. I refer to the first two items: the word of wisdom and the word of knowledge. Are these not the gifts? Never say that in our meetings we do not have the manifestation of the Spirit. We have the manifestation of the best gifts, the first two items of the gifts. What others may have are the last two items. The teaching in today's Christianity is not so accurate, and we have been too influenced by it. We have much of the manifestation of the Spirit in our meetings, yet we have been foolishly influenced to not dare to say that we have the manifestation of the Spirit.

The word of wisdom and the word of knowledge are the first items of the gifts, and tongues and interpretation of tongues are the last items of the gifts. We have the word of wisdom and the word of knowledge in our meetings all the time. Why would we say that we do not have the manifestation of the Spirit? Because of the influence of the traditional teachings of Christianity, we still subconsciously consider that tongues and healings are the gifts. We may never have considered the word of wisdom as the first item of the gifts. In

1 Corinthians 12 through 14 Paul encouraged the Corinthian believers to practice the word of wisdom and the word of knowledge more than tongues. Verse 1 of chapter fourteen says, "Pursue love, and desire earnestly spiritual gifts, but especially that you may prophesy." Verses 4 and 5 say, "He who speaks in a tongue builds up himself, but he who prophesies builds up the church. I desire that you all speak in tongues, but especially that you would prophesy; and greater is he who prophesies than he who speaks in tongues, unless he interprets, that the church may receive building up."

Moreover, not all the Corinthian believers spoke in tongues. If they all did, Paul would have had no need to say, "I desire that you all speak in tongues." This is also a proof that the teaching of today's Charismatic movement is wrong. The Charismatic movement tells people that all have to speak in tongues.

FUNCTIONING IN THE MEETINGS BY PROPHESYING

It is greater to prophesy than to speak in tongues. To prophesy is to exercise the word of wisdom and the word of knowledge. Verses 23 and 24 of chapter fourteen say, "If therefore the whole church comes together in one place, and all speak in tongues, and some unlearned in tongues or unbelievers enter, will they not say that you are insane? But if all prophesy and some unbeliever or unlearned person enters, he is convicted by all, he is examined by all." Verse 23 discourages speaking in tongues, while verse 24 encourages prophesying. In chapters twelve through fourteen of 1 Corinthians Paul's intention was to encourage the believers not to exercise more speaking in tongues but to exercise more of the word of wisdom and the word of knowledge. In this matter we should not follow the traditional teachings. We have to come back to the pure Word.

First Corinthians 12:29 asks, "Are all prophets?", but 14:31 says, "For you can all prophesy one by one that all may learn and all may be encouraged." Not all are prophets, yet Paul says we can all prophesy. This is clear. Forget about the traditional teachings we received from Christianity. They are not accurate. There is a proverb which says, "A little knowledge is dangerous." The traditional teachings we received from Christianity are a little knowledge. They are not adequate. Rather, they are dangerous, so we have to drop them. We must come back to the Bible, the pure Word.

"Each One Has"

Paul's intention in 1 Corinthians 12 and 14 was to encourage us to function in the meetings. In 14:26 he said, "What then, brothers? Whenever you come together, each one has a psalm, has a teaching, has a revelation, has a tongue, has an interpretation. Let all things be done for building up." Each one has. Do not say that you do not have. Many in Christianity teach people to wait until they have an inspiration; without inspiration, one should not take any action in the meetings. Many of us have heard this kind of teaching, but Paul did not say, "Whenever you come together, you must wait until you have the inspiration." Rather, he said, "Each one has." He did not even say, "Each one will have," but "each one has." Each one already has. In 14:26 tongues are not first, but rather a psalm. We may not have a tongue, but we can have a psalm or hymn. Following this he speaks of a teaching and a revelation, then a tongue and an interpretation. However, what each one has is not only of these six items. Again, this list is simply an illustration, and in this illustration Paul put tongues and interpretation as the last items. Tongues and interpretation are always the last items. The first item is a psalm, that is, the singing.

Ministering Christ by Prophesying with Clear and Plain Words

Verses 23 and 24 say, "If therefore the whole church comes together...if all prophesy...." Paul's intention was to encourage us all to function, but not all to speak in tongues. Rather, he expected that all would prophesy. In verse 31 he says, "For you can all prophesy one by one that all may learn and all may be encouraged." To function in the meeting is mainly to prophesy. The traditional teaching of Christianity is strong to tell us that to prophesy is simply to predict, to speak something beforehand. We must understand the meaning of *prophesy* in

1 Corinthians by the whole context of the book. To understand a word in a composition, we have to take care of the context of the whole composition. It is a mistake to define a word in isolation.

Verses 1 and 2 of chapter two say, "And I, when I came to you, brothers, came not according to excellence of speech or of wisdom, announcing to you the mystery of God. For I did not determine to know anything among you except Jesus Christ, and this One crucified." Verse 4 continues, "And my speech and my proclamation were not in persuasive words of wisdom but in demonstration of the Spirit and of power." In these three verses there are two main points. First, Paul determined not to know anything but Christ, and second, his preaching was not with enticing words but in demonstration of the Spirit. Christ and the demonstration of the Spirit are the two main points of these verses. Then, verse 6 of chapter fourteen says, "But now, brothers, if I come to you speaking in tongues, what will I profit you, unless I speak to you either in revelation or in knowledge or in prophecy or in teaching?" By putting all these verses together we can see the way in which Paul functioned in a meeting. He functioned in a meeting by ministering Christ to others. In his ministry he determined to know nothing but Christ, so no doubt the way he functioned was to minister Christ to people. Second, he did not speak in tongues in the meetings. Rather, he spoke the clear and plain word. Third, he spoke by prophesying in the meetings.

To Prophesy Not Mainly Being to Predict

In all the writings of the apostle Paul we can find only a few predictions. Nearly the only predictions in all of Paul's writings are some prophecies of the Lord's coming back (1 Cor. 15:51-52; 1 Thes. 4:15-17; 5:1-3; 2 Thes. 2:1-10). Today in the Pentecostal or charismatic meetings there are many predictions. Many such prophecies begin with, "Yea My people, thus saith the Lord." When I came to this country, I was surprised to learn that regardless what language the speaker used, whether Chinese, Filipino, or English, the tone of this kind of speaking was the same, and the wording was nearly the same. To prophesy in the New Testament does not mainly mean to predict. In the entire book of Acts there are only two predictions. In chapter eleven there was a prediction that there would be a famine over the whole inhabited earth (vv. 27-30), and in 21:8-11 one predicted that Paul would be arrested and bound if he went to Jerusalem. In all the Epistles of the apostles there are nearly no predictions other than certain prophecies of the coming back of the Lord Jesus.

The Problem of False Predictions

In the charismatic meetings there are predictions after predictions. Nearly all these predictions were never fulfilled. In 1963 on the West Coast I saw a mimeographed booklet with a prophecy that there would be a great earthquake in the following year which would cause Los Angeles to go down into the ocean. The prophecy warned people to go to the mountains to dig caves to live in. Some took the warning and moved away, but 1964 came and nothing happened. Then after 1964 they predicted the same thing again. This prediction was even put into the newspapers in Los Angeles and San Francisco. People talked much about it, but nothing happened. The tongue-speaking movement along the West Coast was very much cooled down by this false prophecy. People were no longer fooled by it.

In a certain city this kind of movement became active among us. It was prevailing to the extent that the leading ones in the church there came to me about it. I told them, "There is no other way than to go to the Lord. Call on the Head as the authority. Let the Lord vindicate His way." They prayed in this way, and something happened. The prevailing one in this kind of prophesying was a sister. One day a dear sister among us suddenly died of tuberculosis. She was a lovely sister, and the whole church loved her. The prevailing, tongue-speaking sister immediately made a prediction and told the husband not to prepare a funeral. She said the sister would be resurrected the following day at noon. This false prophecy was devilish. On the next day before noontime all the saints crowded into that house to see the resurrection. The sister who prophesied went into the room with two elders to pray desperately. Then noontime came and nothing happened. By three o'clock still nothing had happened. Then one of the three elders said, "Brothers and sisters, we should no longer listen to this. Let us prepare a funeral for our sister." The husband agreed to this. The brother sent certain ones to prepare a place and buy a coffin, and the crowd left. That was the end of this movement. The whole church was rescued, and all the saints came back to the regular meetings of the church.

The Scriptural Meaning of Prophesying

In the New Testament and in the whole Bible, prophesying first means to tell for, to speak something for, the Lord. Second it is to tell forth, to make a declaration. Third it is to foretell, to tell beforehand. The latter is a prediction, but this is not the main meaning of prophesying. To prophesy mainly means to tell for or tell forth. This is not only so in the New Testament Epistles; it is also so with the Old Testament prophets such as Isaiah and Jeremiah. Isaiah contains much telling for and telling forth the Lord, although, of course, there is also some foretelling. It is difficult to find many predictions in the New Testament, but there is much telling, speaking something for the Lord Jesus, and much telling forth, declaring something to people about the Lord's doing. There is relatively little of the third kind of prophesying.

Based upon this, we may see what it is to prophesy in the meetings. It is to speak something for the Lord, to tell forth something of the Lord. A brother should stand up and strongly say, "Praise the Lord! Today the Lord Jesus has been constantly my strength." This is to prophesy. The brother tells something for the Lord Jesus, and at the same time he also tells forth, he declares something about the Lord Jesus. Then a sister may stand up and say, "Hallelujah! Today Jesus was my Lord in my kitchen." This is both telling for and telling forth. This is the proper prophecy.

We cannot pick up a word such as *prophesy* in an isolated way to define it. This is dangerous. We have to take care of the whole context of 1 Corinthians. This book tells us that Paul the apostle, as an example of functioning in the meetings, determined not to know anything but Christ, and he did this with a strong spirit, a demonstration of the Spirit, not in an unknown tongue but in clear words. He said, "But in the church I would rather speak five words with my mind, that I might instruct others also, than ten thousand words in a tongue" (14:19). This is the proper way to prophesy in the meetings.

To be sure, we can all prophesy in this way. If to prophesy were to predict something, I am afraid that throughout the whole year none of us would prophesy. We would come together again and again, waiting for inspiration, but no inspiration would come. Eventually, we would be forced to make some false predictions such as of a great earthquake in Los Angeles. To prophesy in the meetings is simply to tell something for the Lord, to tell forth something about the Lord. We must declare to the universe, to all the principalities and powers in the heavenly places, that the Lord Jesus is our life. Today He was with us all the time, in our kitchen, our dining room, our living room, and even when we went shopping. This is prophesying. It is so simple, yet so practical and profitable.

If we pray-read all the verses in this message and review all the points which we have covered and put them into practice, we will see something. When we come together, it is wonderful to speak something for Christ by exercising our spirit. We say something for Christ with the demonstration of the Spirit, not in a weak, timid way, but in a strong way. We have a strong spirit, so living and so aggressive, and we have some experiences of Christ to tell others. We do have something of Christ to speak about, to declare. Therefore, when we come to the meeting, we exercise our spirit to say something for Christ, to say something about Christ. You say something. I say something. Everybody says something. This will have a convincing impact on others.

CHAPTER TWELVE

CALLING ON THE LORD IN OUR DAILY LIFE FOR THE CHURCH MEETINGS

Scripture Reading: 1 Cor. 1:2, 24; 5:7b-8; 12:13, 3b, 31; 13:1; 14:1, 5, 23-26, 31-32, 39; 15:45b; 2 Cor. 3:17; 1 Cor. 2:14-15

First Corinthians may be considered the richest, most wonderful book in the New Testament. It covers the Christian daily life and the church meetings. If we wish to know how a Christian must live day by day, we have to come to this book. Likewise, if we seek to know how the church has to meet, we have to come to this book. In no other book are these two matters—the Christian daily life and the church meetings—more fully and adequately covered. I am afraid that many have read this book for years without seeing these two matters. They have been distracted by certain points in it. As we have pointed out, this book deals with eleven great problems. For this reason many are unable to pick up the main points when they read this book. When they get into this book, they become distracted, puzzled, and even perplexed by these eleven great problems. However, the secret to reading 1 Corinthians is to not care for the problems. With Christ and the church there is no problem.

Someone may say, "I don't believe there is no problem. The more I come to the church, the more problems I have." If this is so, it means that he has not yet entered into the church. When we enter in, there are no more problems. There is only Christ and the cross. The cross is the biggest, most prevailing, and most effective "germicide" for our problems. It can kill any kind of "germ," even such a great "germ" as the devil. Today in modern medicine there are many kinds of medicines, but we have only one kind of medicine—the cross. When we get into the church life, there are no problems because we have the cross of Christ as the antibiotic, something that is always killing. Paul said, "For I did not determine to know anything among you except Jesus Christ, and this One crucified" (1 Cor. 2:2), that is, Christ and the cross. Hallelujah, if we have the cross, what problems can we have? If we take just one "dose" of the cross, everything is fine. Do not be bothered by the problems. In the church life there is no problem.

THE CHURCH OF GOD WHICH IS IN CORINTH

First Corinthians is wonderful. This wonderful book starts in a wonderful way. No other book of the sixty-six books in the Bible starts in such a way. It starts with "to the church of God" (1:2a). Today many Christians do not pay attention to the church. They speak of certain kinds of churches, not the church of God. But 1:2 speaks of the church of God which is in a locality, Corinth, like the church in Chicago, Atlanta, or Detroit. This is not a church in theory, a church "in the air," but a church on this earth, and not only on this earth but in a locality. This expression is so definite. We all must have such a church, a church of God on this earth and in our locality.

THE SANCTIFIED AND CALLED SAINTS

Moreover, the persons in this church are sanctified and called, not called sinners or even called believers, but called saints. The word *saints* means the holy ones. Do you believe that you are a holy one? In the Catholic Church and even in some of the denominations, especially the Church of England, certain ones are referred to as saints, such as Saint Paul. When we hear people refer to Saint Paul, we have to tell them that we also are a saint. We all are called saints. In the church everyone is a saint. We may believe that the Corinthian believers must have been marvelous to be called saints. However, the following verses speak of divisions (vv. 11-12), and chapter three speaks of jealousy and strife, saying that they were still infants and were not only fleshly but fleshy (3:1, 3). Still, they were called saints. Praise the Lord, we are the called saints!

BEING CALLED TO CALL ON THE LORD

Verse 2 of chapter one continues to say, "With all those who call upon the name of our Lord Jesus Christ." We have to call upon the name of the Lord. We have been called to call. We are the called ones, and we are the calling ones. As to our position we are the called ones; as to our situation we are the calling ones. Day by day we call, saying, "O Lord Jesus! O Lord Jesus! Jesus Lord!" We are the calling ones, all the time making a cry. Even when we visit our relatives, we have to be the calling ones, all the day calling on the name of the Lord Jesus.

OUR CALLING ON THE LORD BEING OUR BREATHING

To call on the Lord is to enjoy the Lord, to breathe the Lord in. Calling is just breathing. Jeremiah was designated the "weeping prophet." After the book of Jeremiah, he felt he was not finished, so he wrote Lamentations as a weeping book. In this weeping book there are two wonderful, joyful verses: "I called upon Your name, O Jehovah, / From the lowest pit. / You have heard my voice; do not hide / Your ear at my breathing, at my cry" (3:55-56). Our calling is our breathing. We have to call on the name of the Lord because to call on the Lord is to breathe. Sometimes our dear husband or wife or our children put us into "the lowest pit." Whenever you get into "the lowest pit," do not murmur or complain. Simply call, "O Lord Jesus," and you will be in the third heaven. To call on the Lord is just to breathe Him in. Verse 56 says, "Do not hide / Your ear at my breathing, at my cry." The Lord turns His ear to our breathing. This spiritual breathing is our calling, "O Lord Jesus, O Lord Jesus."

To call on the Lord is to take the Lord in. First Corinthians 15:45b is a very important verse which tells us, "The last Adam became a life-giving Spirit." *Spirit* in Greek is *pneuma,* the word for breath. Therefore, this verse may be translated as, "The last Adam became a life-giving Breath." Today Christ is the Breath, the Air, the Spirit, the life-giving *Pneuma* so we can breathe Him in. The way to participate in Christ and enjoy Him is to call on Him. Because He is the Breath, to call on Him is to breathe Him as the Breath into us.

Whenever we feel lonely, we should call on the Lord. Right away we will have the sensation that the Lord is with us. The more we call on Him, the more He is with us and the more we enjoy His presence. This is because the Lord is the Breath. When we breathe deeply by calling on the Lord, we have a refreshing sensation within. To call "O Lord Jesus" is refreshing and spiritually enjoyable because when we call on the Lord, we breathe Him in. He is the Breath; He is the Air; He is the life-giving Spirit.

OUR CALLING BEING THE KEY
FOR ENTERING INTO THE RICHES OF CHRIST

First Corinthians clearly tells us that Christ is the power of God and the wisdom of God to the called ones (1:24). He is also the Passover and the Feast of Unleavened Bread (5:7b-8). The only way to enjoy such a Christ is to call on Him. This book is in the hands of all Christians, and I believe most Christians have read it. Very few, however, have seen the matter of calling on the Lord. We all must know that this is the key to get into the riches of the Lord. If we have not seen calling on the Lord, we do not have the key. This may be compared to having a wonderful building but no key. We can appreciate the building, but we cannot enter into it. In Christianity certain teachers teach people that unto us, both Jews and Greeks, Christ is the power of God and the wisdom of God. Such teachers may present a picture of a wonderful "building," but where is the entrance? Most of them do not know. People may talk much about Christ as power and wisdom, but how can we get into Christ? The key to entering into such a Christ is to call, "O Lord Jesus!"

The fundamentalist teaching in Christianity tells us that as long as we believe in Christ, we are in Christ and we have everything. Fundamentalist teaching is objective. It is wonderful, but merely "in the air." The Pentecostal teaching tells us that we have nothing until we speak in tongues. Nothing is ours; we even have not been saved and regenerated. Therefore, we have to pray, seek, fast, and wait until some great power falls upon us, and then we start to turn our tongue, exercise our jaw, and speak anything but English. Neither teaching is accurate. The fundamentalist teachings are too much at one extreme, and the Pentecostal teachings are too much at the other extreme. We have to come back from both extremes. Forget about the Pentecostal teachings and forget about the fundamentalist teachings. Come back to the pure word of the Bible.

The pure Word says that the Lord is "rich to all who call upon Him" (Rom. 10:12). It is so easy. If we just call on the Lord, all the riches of Christ are ours. There is no doubt about this, but we have to participate. The manna comes down from heaven, but we have to go and pick it up. In the morning someone may serve us breakfast, but we have to go to the table and use our hands and mouth to eat. We cannot say that because everything is on the table, it is ours. The more we say it is good enough that it is on the table, the more it is not enough. After we say, "Good enough," for ten days, we will be ready for a funeral. We need to eat. Yes, all the riches of Christ are ours, but we may not participate in them. There is much on the table, but only that which we take into us is really ours. There may be thirty pounds of beef on the table, but if we eat only two and a half ounces, only that much is ours. We have to participate and eat.

The way to eat Jesus and participate in Him is to call, "O Lord Jesus!" There is no other way. Romans 10:12 does not say that the Lord is rich unto all that merely believe on Him. Merely to believe on Him is not enough. If we only believe that a meal which has been prepared for us is good, the cook may say, "Silly brothers, I don't care to see that you believe. I like to see that you eat. I don't care whether you believe this food is good or not. I don't care even if you complain. As long as you eat, that is good enough." Merely to believe in the Lord and to love Him does not work. Only one thing works: to call, "O Lord Jesus!" Try to call in this way. To be sure, this will cause us to reject all the fundamentalist teachings. We may tell others, "I don't care for this teaching. I only care for calling, 'O Lord Jesus!'" After calling for ten minutes, we may tell the Pentecostal teachers, "I don't need to wait, and I don't need to fast. After calling on the name of the Lord for ten minutes, I can go to breakfast, because I have enjoyed Him." Regardless of whether you are old or young, I would challenge and encourage you all to do this. Try it tomorrow morning for ten minutes. After calling on the Lord for ten minutes, you will be on fire. Hallelujah, we have the entrance, and we have the key! This little key truly works. The Lord is rich to all who call upon Him!

First Corinthians 1:2b says "With all those who call upon the name of our Lord Jesus Christ in every place, who is theirs and ours." Christ is our portion, yours and mine. The way to participate in our portion is by calling on Him. This is wonderful. By calling in this way we are truly feasting, not fasting, day by day. Our Christian life is a feasting life. Day by day we enjoy Christ as a feast.

ALL BEING BAPTIZED IN ONE SPIRIT

First Corinthians 12:13 says, "For also in one Spirit we were all baptized into one Body, whether Jews or Greeks, whether slaves or free, and were all given to drink one Spirit." Listen to the pure Word; do not listen to any other word. The Pentecostals often ask if we have been baptized in the Holy Spirit. From now on whenever someone asks this, we should answer, "Have you not read 1 Corinthians 12:13?" Do not listen to man's teaching; listen to the pure Word. Here is a verse telling us that we all were baptized. *All* included all the Corinthians, but in 14:5 Paul says, "I desire that you all speak in tongues." This indicates that some of the Corinthians had not spoken in tongues. All the Corinthians were baptized in the Holy Spirit, but at least some of the Corinthians had never spoken in tongues. Do not listen to the traditional teachings of today's Christianity, whether they are Pentecostal or fundamentalist. Come back to the pure Word. Whether or not we have spoken in tongues, as long as we believe in the Lord Jesus, we were baptized in the Spirit.

ALL BEING GIVEN TO DRINK ONE SPIRIT

First Corinthians 12:13 mentions something besides the baptism in the Holy Spirit. We need this balance. The last part of the verse says, "And were all given to drink one Spirit."

We all have been baptized in the Holy Spirit. This is one matter, but there is another: We all have been given to drink. God can only give us to drink, but He cannot drink for us. Now we have to drink. We were all baptized in one Spirit, but I doubt that we are all now drinking. The pure Word tells us that as long as we believe in the Lord Jesus, we all have been baptized in the Spirit, whether we are Jews or Gentiles, slaves or free. But following this we also have been given, positioned, to drink. Whether or not we drink is up to us. In the morning I am made to eat by being positioned at the dining table. However, suppose I only sat there and said, "Hallelujah, I have been positioned to eat." My host may say, "Now is not the time for you to talk. Now is the time for you to eat. Forget that you have been positioned and simply eat." Today is not the time to be baptized. We have been baptized already. Today is for us to drink.

To be baptized is to be put into the water. To drink is to take the water in. We cannot replace taking the water in with being put into the water. These are two different matters. If a brother is thirsty and I only baptize him, he may say, "Be merciful to me. I don't need so much water. I just want one glass. Don't put me into the water. Rather, give me a little water to drink." Baptism can never replace drinking. In Christianity many only talk about baptism. They never talk about drinking. But in 1 Corinthians 12:13 there are both matters, and between these two is the conjunction *and*. We all were baptized *and* we all were given to drink. Baptism is no problem; it has already been accomplished. Praise the Lord, we also have been positioned to drink, but the Lord can never drink for us. For eternity we have to drink.

The way to drink is in verse 3 of the same chapter: "No one can say, Jesus is Lord! except in the Holy Spirit." This is similar to saying, "No one can breathe except that the air gets into him." Can we say that we are breathing, but the air never comes in? When we breathe, the air comes in. If we open up our mouth and exercise to breathe, the air comes in. If we say, "O Lord Jesus!", we are in the Spirit. This is drinking. The way we drink of the Spirit is by saying, "O Lord Jesus."

As we have seen already from Lamentations, our calling,

"O Lord Jesus," is our breathing. Hymn #73 in *Hymns* was written by Miss M. E. Barber, an older sister who helped Brother Watchman Nee very much. Stanza 2 says, "Blessed Jesus! Mighty Savior! / In Thy Name is all I need; / Just to breathe the Name of Jesus, / Is to drink of Life indeed." Three or four years ago when I told the Lord's people that to breathe is to drink, I was a little doubtful. I had never heard anyone say this, and I thought that I might be too much. However, one night in Los Angeles this hymn was called. While we were singing, I was surprised at the lines which say, "Just to breathe the Name of Jesus, / Is to drink of Life indeed." At least one other person, Miss Barber, a sister who was deep in the Lord, experienced the same thing. To call on the name of the Lord is to breathe Him, and to breathe Him is to drink of Him. The way to drink of the one Spirit is to call, "O Lord Jesus!" To call is to breathe, and to breathe is to drink, so to call is simply to drink. If you are thirsty, call on the Lord. At any time or any place, even while we are driving, we may be thirsty. Then we may call on the Lord and receive the living water. Try it; it always works. When we call on the name of the Lord, we drink of the Lord and we receive all the riches of the Lord.

There is no need for anyone to teach, instruct, or correct us. If a brother has long hair and is unshaven, no one may ever tell him to cut his hair or shave, but if every day he would call, "O Lord Jesus," some "cutting scissors" would come to him from within. The only problem is that we may not drink; we may not call on the name of the Lord. Sometimes I have been put into a situation in which I was about to lose my temper. My temper was on fire. However, after calling, "O Lord Jesus!", three times, the fire was quenched. To call on the Lord in this way is marvelous. If someone gives me a difficult time, I may feel badly toward him. If a pastor would come and try to instruct me not to lose my temper, I may lose my temper all the more and even become angry at the pastor. However, if I would call on the Lord three times, I will love that person. All we need is Jesus, and the way to participate in Jesus is by calling on Him. The Lord is "rich to all who call upon Him." This is very simple, and this is our Christian life. Our Christian life must be a calling life.

BUILDING UP THE CHURCH
BY PROPHESYING WITH A LIVING SPIRIT

Acts 9:14 says that Paul received authority from the chief priests to go to Damascus to cast into prison all who called on the name of the Lord. The ancient believers were the calling ones. We also have to call on the Lord day by day. The more we call, the more we gain, enjoy, and experience Christ, and the more Christ we have. Then when we come to the meeting, we come with Christ. We come in a bubbling way, and we are full of Christ. We may come, saying, "Oh, Christ is so good! Christ is so sweet. Christ is so dear! Christ is so precious! Christ is powerful, mighty, and living, and He is everything to me." Not only so, but we also come to the meeting with a strong spirit, with a spirit that is living, active, and aggressive, and we want to say something. We are not able to keep silent. We open up our mouth and release our spirit, and Christ comes out. We say something for Christ and minister Him to others.

To speak in this way is to prophesy, as mentioned in 1 Corinthians 14. In 1 Corinthians *prophesy* does not mainly mean to predict. To prophesy is to speak something for Christ, to speak something about Christ, and to minister Christ to others. This is why Paul says, "For you can all prophesy" (v. 31).

PARTICIPATING IN CHRIST AND
COMING TO THE MEETINGS WITH CHRIST

A dumb Christian is one who never calls on the Lord. Rather, he always exercises his mind, perhaps to consider some verses of the Bible and afterward to consider the elders and the other brothers. Such a one always exercises his mind day by day and does not enjoy Christ. He has much deadness and many negative things within him. Then when he comes to the meeting, he comes empty, with no Christ. His spirit is down, but his eyes are open. When he examines the brothers, not one is good to him, and when he looks at the sisters, he considers that every one is worldly. With some, their hair is too long, and with others, their skirts are too short. He looks at the whole situation with much criticism and condemnation. Such a one is deadened and is deadening to the whole situation, and he kills the meeting. If anyone speaks, he does not agree with him. He may say, "This one is not eloquent, that one has an accent, and none of them is good." He may think that he is the best one, but in actuality he is deadened. This is the situation in Christianity today. There is very little life and ministry of Christ. For this reason, people feel they must hire a pastor, train a choir, and bring in a soloist to sing. May the Lord be merciful to us, and may we come out of this situation!

The right way for us to meet is first to have the experience of the first eleven chapters of 1 Corinthians, to have a proper life by participating in Christ. We all have to have such a calling life. All day we call upon the Lord, we enjoy Him, and we live by Him. "He who eats Me, he also shall live because of Me" (John 6:57). We eat the Lord Jesus, we drink Him, and we live by Him, for Him, and with Him. We are filled with Him, full of Christ, and our spirit is strong, living, and aggressive. When we come to the meeting, we do not see anything negative. We are only filled with Christ, and we are bubbling! If everyone would be like this, what kind of meeting we will have! The meeting will ascend to the third heaven. To have the full release of the spirit is the right way to meet, but this needs the proper Christian life in our daily walk.

LIVING BY CHRIST AND FUNCTIONING WITH CHRIST

Then when we come into the meeting, we do not wait; we do not depend on any speaker. Rather, we all function. One has a psalm, one has a revelation, another has a word for Jesus, and another has a testimony. Everyone functions; all prophesy. What a rich meeting this is!

Paul said, "If therefore the whole church comes together in one place, and all speak in tongues, and some unlearned in tongues or unbelievers enter, will they not say that you are insane? But if all prophesy and some unbeliever or unlearned person enters, he is convicted by all, he is examined by all" (1 Cor. 14:23-24). In verse 31 he said, "For you can all prophesy." This means we can all speak something for Christ, and by so doing, the church will be built up and all the "germs" will be killed. There will be no criticism, no gossip, and no murmuring. Rather, all will be praising, shouting, and saying, "Hallelujah!" We will be full of Christ, and the church will be built up. This is not a matter of the gifts, nor a matter of the teachings, but a matter of eating Jesus, living by Jesus, and then meeting with Jesus. We all come together with Christ. Christ is our life in our daily walk, and Christ is our function, our ministry, in our meetings. In this way the church is built up.

The words *church* and *churches* are used nine times in chapter fourteen, and *build, built,* and *building* are used seven times. God's intention is to build up the church, and the way to build the church is by our meeting together. The more we meet, the more the church is built up. However, we need something to meet with; we need Christ in our daily walk. Day by day we live by Christ, we enjoy Christ, we experience Christ, we gain Christ, we are filled with Christ, and we are full of Christ. Then we have Christ to meet with.

COMING TO THE MEETING
FULL OF CHRIST IN DEMONSTRATION OF THE SPIRIT

Christ is our life in our daily walk, and this life is mainly expressed in love (ch. 13). Love is the expression of life. Love is the outward expression, and life is the inward reality. We all have Christ within as our life, and this life is expressed in love. Therefore, we all love one another, not in a fleshly way but in the spirit. We love, and this love is the expression of the inner life, and this inner life is simply Christ. Therefore, we have Christ and we are full of Christ. Then we come to the meeting with Christ. We meet with Christ. We have something of Christ to meet with, and we have a strong spirit. Whenever we say something, we say it in the spirit. Whenever we sing, we sing in the spirit. We have the demonstration of our spirit with all the riches of Christ. It is by this way that the church is built up. This is not merely a doctrine, a theory, or a theology. This is a fact, a reality, and a practicality. We have seen this clearly in the church in Los Angeles, and now we are seeing it in many local churches.

THE EXTRACT OF 1 CORINTHIANS

What we have spoken here is the extract of 1 Corinthians. We all have to realize that today our Christ is the life-giving Spirit (15:45b; 2 Cor. 3:17a), and we are one spirit with Him (1 Cor. 6:17). He is the life-giving Spirit, we have a regenerated spirit, and these two spirits are mingled together. We are one spirit with the Lord. Now we need to learn to walk in the spirit. We must never walk in the soul, never be soulish but be spiritual (2:14-15). We walk in the spirit day by day, enjoying Christ. Then when we come to the meetings, we come with a strong spirit with all the riches of Christ. We take the initiative to say something, and our spirit goes along with us. Our spirit is subject to us (14:32). This is marvelous. First Corinthians is a book of Christ as our life in our daily walk and Christ as our function, our ministry, in our meetings for the building up of the church. The church is built in this way.

CHAPTER THIRTEEN

THE UNIQUE ONENESS
FOR THE BUILDING OF THE CHURCH

Scripture Reading: John 10:16; 17:21-23; 1 Cor. 1:5, 7a, 10-13, 22-24; 2:1-2; Eph. 4:3-6; Titus 3:10

In the previous chapters we saw the building of God. Every building must have a site. Without a site building is impossible. In this chapter we will see what the site for the building up of the church is. In the New Testament the unique site for building the church is the unique oneness. This unique oneness is the site, the ground, for us to build the church.

ONENESS IN LIFE, NATURE, POSITION, AND EXPRESSION IN THE GOSPEL OF JOHN

The Folds and One Flock

Both the Gospels and the Epistles speak about the oneness. The first mention of oneness in the New Testament is by the Lord Himself in John 10:16, which says, "And I have other sheep, which are not of this fold; I must lead them also, and they shall hear My voice, and there shall be one flock, one Shepherd." The King James Version renders the latter part of verse 16 as, "there shall be one fold, and one shepherd." The latter mention of the word *fold* in this verse is actually the word *flock* in Greek. A fold is a place which holds the flock. It has nothing to do with life. It is a place of shelter or a fenced area to protect the flock. The flock, however, is not a place. The flock is something living. The flock is the collection of all the sheep.

Today the wrong teaching in traditional Christianity says that the church is a fold. For example, we say that a backslider is a person who is away from the fold. This teaching is absolutely wrong. A fold is a religion. Judaism was a fold. Before the Lord Jesus came, God used the law as a fold to hold His people (Gal. 3:23). When the Lord Jesus came, however, He opened the door of the law, the door of Judaism, not only for people to go in but also for them to come out.

Christ Being the Door In and Out of the Fold

John 10:9 says, "I am the door; if anyone enters through Me, he shall be saved and shall go in and go out and shall find pasture." We have to be very careful in dealing with the Lord's Word. The order of the words in this verse is very important. It says that the saved one will "go in and go out." What does *go in* mean? Some have said that this is going into heaven. If this were true, then the phrase *go out* which follows means that someone can go out of heaven.

The door in verse 9 is not the door to the heavens. When I was young, I was taught that Jesus in John 10 was the door for us to enter into the heavens, but this is absolutely a wrong teaching. In John 10, Jesus is not the door of the heavens; He is the door of the fold which is Judaism.

Before the Lord Jesus came, God used the law as a fold to hold His people. Even in the Old Testament, Christ was the door for God's people to enter into the fold. David, Isaiah, Jeremiah, and all of the prophets entered the fold through Christ. They were God's people, God's sheep. In the Old Testament, Christ was the door for all God's people to go into Judaism to be held there. Then in John 10, Christ came as the door for all these sheep to come out of the fold of Judaism. Christ was the door for His people to go in, and He is the door for His people to come out. First we go into the fold, and then we go out.

Out of Many Folds into One Flock

In verse 16 the Lord Jesus said, "And I have other sheep, which are not of this fold." Outside the Jewish religion God has other sheep—the Gentile believers. God has His chosen people among the Gentiles. They, as well as those in Judaism, are His sheep. The Lord brings these two groups of sheep not into one fold but into one flock.

Judaism is a fold, and today nearly all of the denominations also are folds. Today the Lord Jesus is the door, not for us to go into the heavens but for us to get out of the denominations. The Lord Jesus is the door out of the fold. The church, however, is not a fold. The church is not a place; the church is a living Body, a living collection of the sheep. Therefore, the church is the flock.

The flock needs the fold at nighttime, in the wintertime, or during a storm. At such times the flock needs a shelter. That is the function of the fold. But in the daytime, in the springtime, or in a peaceful time, the flock does not stay in the fold. During such times the flock goes out of the fold and into the pasture. The pasture is Christ. Christ is both the door and the pasture. Christ is the door for us to leave the fold to enjoy the pasture, which is also Christ Himself.

Are you in the night, in the wintertime, or in a stormy time? Today I can testify that I am not in the night; I am in the day. I am not in the wintertime; I am in the springtime. Therefore, I do not need any fold. Jesus was my door, and I have come out of the fold by Jesus. Now I am in the pasture feeding on Jesus. This is a picture of the church. The church is not a fold; the church is a flock. This flock is in the pasture feeding on and masticating the tender grass. Every meeting of a local church is a feeding on the green and tender grass. We are in the pasture, not in a classroom or in a fold.

If we remain in the folds, how can we be one? In John 10:16 the Lord Jesus said that He had other sheep which were not of that fold. This means that in addition to the fold of Judaism there were other folds. There are many folds, but the flock is one. Today I am not in the fold; I am in the pasture. Where are you? If you are in the fold, you are divided from me. Some may turn this charge to me and say, "No, you are divided from me." I may be divided from you, but it is because I am in the pasture. To be separate from others by being in the pasture is right, but to be divided from others by being in the folds is wrong. If we are in one of the folds, we are wrong. If we are in the pasture, we are right.

Oneness By Life

How can we be one? John 10:10 says, "I have come that they may have life and may have it abundantly." The Lord Jesus did not say that He came that they might have knowledge, teachings, speaking in tongues, the gift of healing, or all the other gifts. He said, "I have come that they may have life."

In the oldness of Judaism, there were many things, including the law, letters, doctrines, knowledge, and the Ten Commandments. But in John 10, Jesus is so simple; with Him there is only life. We can be one only by the life of Jesus. If we try to be one by the law, you may be for the first commandment, and I may be for the second commandment; another brother may be for the third commandment, and still another brother may be for the fourth commandment. If there are ten brothers, we may all be divided into ten individual groups because we all have different opinions about the Ten Commandments.

In Jesus, however, how many lives are there? There is only one life in Jesus. It is impossible to be one by the Ten Commandments, doctrines, or teachings. The more we get into the law, the teachings, or the commandments, the more we are divided. The more we are in the life of Jesus, however, the more we are one. In the life of Jesus, there are no opinions, but if we care for anything other than life, we will be divided and divisive. According to the context of John 10, the way to be one flock is by Christ being life to us.

Dropping the Divisive Things and Coming Back to Christ

In the spring of 1963 after I was first sent by the Lord to minister in the United States, I was invited to speak to three Brethren assemblies. The Brethren assemblies have been divided into many divisions. The Brethren started the church life in 1828, but after only ninety years, they were divided into one hundred fifty divisions. From that time until today there have been even more divisions. Today there may be a thousand divisions among the Brethren. One Brethren assembly was divided over the playing of the piano. Some insisted on using a piano, while others opposed the use of a piano. Eventually, that assembly was divided into two assemblies. When I spoke with those assemblies, I was very bold to tell them that they needed to drop all their teachings. I said, "The reason that you are so divided is that you take care only of teachings and opinions. You must drop all the doctrines and come back to Christ as life." This offended them, so immediately after my message some of them rebuked me to my face. I do not want to be a troublemaker, but I have a real burden concerning the oneness.

If we all are for life, we are one, but if we are for doctrines, gifts, or anything other than life, we will be divided. We are here only for life. The Lord Jesus said that He came that we might have life and have it more abundantly. This is so that we can be one flock. We can be flocked together by Christ as our life, not by anything else. This is very clear.

Jesus is the door, not for us to go into heaven, but for us to come out of anything that holds us back from the church. Jesus is the door to release us, to set us free, from all kinds of folds. Then after we come out of the fold, He is not only our life but also our pasture and our Shepherd (vv. 9-11). He is the door, He is the pasture, He is the life, and He is the Shepherd. Today we are out of many folds to be in the flock, the church. We are the flock by the life of Jesus, and as the flock we are feeding on Jesus as the green pasture.

Oneness in the Divine Life and Nature
with the Divine Position to Express the Father

In John 17 the Lord prayed that we all would be one (vv. 11, 21-23). In what way can we all be one? Verse 22 says, "And the glory which You have given Me I have given to them, that they may be one, even as We are one." The glory that the Father gave to the Son is the divine life with the divine nature plus the divine position for the Son to express the Father. This glory has been given to us by the Son. Now we have the divine life, the divine nature, and the divine position. This is ours by our divine birth, by being born again. As children of God, we have the divine life, the divine nature, and the divine position to express the Father.

If we all would drop our concepts and simply be for the divine life, the divine nature, and the divine position to express the Father, we all would be one. We can never be one by doctrines. We can never be one by opinions. Two brothers may have differing opinions about everything. One brother may think that the other brother's hair is too long, while the other brother thinks that the first brother's hair is too short. One brother thinks that the other should shave, but the other brother thinks that to shave too often is worldly. One brother feels that everyone should wear a tie to the meetings, while the other brother feels that this is too worldly because Jesus never wore a tie. We all have our opinions, so what shall we do? We must drop our opinions. The way to drop our opinions is by taking Christ as life. Without taking Christ as life, we may drop one opinion and pick up another opinion. We will have one opinion after another. We must drop the opinions and come back to the glory that the Lord Jesus has given us. This glory is the divine life, the divine nature, and the divine position to express the Father. Hallelujah, we have God's life, we have God's nature, and we have the position as God's children to express Him. This is our glory. If we care only for this glory, we all are one. Long hair or short hair, wide neckties or narrow neckties, shaving or not shaving—all these things make no difference.

Perfected into One

John 17:23 says, "I in them, and You in Me, that they may be perfected into one." In what way can we be perfected? In our old nature we are not one. We can be perfected into one only by Jesus being in us. The Lord Jesus is within us. He is in you, He is in me, and He is in every one of His believers. By His being in us, we are being perfected.

If you say that my hair is too short, I may say that your hair is too long; then we will fight. We should forget about the length of our hair. Let us talk about Jesus. If I say to a brother, "Your hair is too long," his response should be, "Brother, don't you know that Jesus is within you? Don't talk to me about hair. Talk to me about Jesus." To be sure, if we talk about anything other than Jesus, eventually we will be divided. If someone asks you about tongue-speaking, do not answer him. You may say, "Brother, don't you know that Jesus is within you? Let's change the subject and talk about Jesus." If we talk about tongue-speaking for ten minutes, we will be divided. You may be for it, and I may be against it. Who is right and who is wrong? Only the Lord knows. We simply need to be perfected into one.

To speak doctrinally about loving one another is very easy, but when we are put together practically, what happens to our love for one another? Immediately we may be exposed because we are still too natural. If we are natural with one another, it is impossible for us to be one. Therefore, we must be perfected, not by being regulated, but by enjoying the indwelling Christ.

When I was a young Christian, I once stayed in a small bedroom with an older brother. Sometimes as I brought water in a basin into the room, I would spill a little water on his bed. Then I would go to him, confess, and ask for his forgiveness. After a few days of this, he said, "Brother, it is better to not do anything wrong and need to confess." This caused me to be anxious, but the more careful I was, the more water I spilled and the more I needed to confess. This illustrates that to stay together with others is not easy. One day, however, we all will be perfected, not by being regulated but by realizing that Christ is in us. Real oneness is in the indwelling Christ.

CARING FOR CHRIST AND NOT OUTWARD THINGS

I am concerned for some who still hold certain concepts and ideas about the Christian meetings. Some may consider that Christian meetings should be orderly and dignified. They may say, "Look at these people. They are shouting and laughing. There is no dignity with them." I do not like to criticize those who say this, but I would say that dignity is not Christ. Today we all have to consider Christ. We must not care for anything but Christ. We may say that we do not like a certain kind of meeting because it is too noisy, but what if the Lord

Jesus likes it? The Lord Jesus may say, "I am happy. They may not be so good, but they are living while others are dead."

Why are Christians divided and still being divided? It is because they hold many good things other than Christ. To be orderly and to have dignity is good. I do not like to see careless shouting and laughing, and I do not like to see wild and uncivilized long hair and beards. I would rather see everyone with a proper haircut, properly shaven, and dressed with a proper tie. However, we have to look into the deeper situation. For someone to have a tie makes no difference if he does not have much Christ.

The Lord Jesus did not usually have meetings in orderly places. He had meetings on the seashore, on the hillside, or on the mountaintops. In those meetings, there was no chair arranging or cleaning beforehand. Almost every meeting was a mess. The exception was when the Lord fed the five thousand; He had them sit down in groups of fifty (Luke 9:14). To meet in this way was the Lord's wisdom in order to distribute food to the people. It was a matter of wisdom, not a matter of dignity. The Lord Jesus did not care for mere outward dignity and order.

Two centuries ago John Wesley was raised up by the Lord. In England at that time no one was allowed to preach the word of God outside of a building dedicated by the Church of England to be a "sanctuary." Their thought was that the word of God is so holy that it should be preached only in a sanctuary, a holy place, and not in a common place. However, God raised up John Wesley. Wesley did not care for the concept of the sanctuary. He preached the word of God on the street corners. This kind of preaching eventually became one of the biggest revivals of recent times.

The Lord Jesus does not care for mere outward things. He cares only for Himself, that is, for how much Christ we have. We all need to be perfected into one. If we care only for Christ, we will not care for an outward way to have our meetings. Whether the meeting is noisy or quiet, orderly or disorderly, full of dignity or without any dignity, makes no difference to us. If we care only for Christ, we will have no opinion because we are being perfected into one by and with Christ. There is no other way for us to be one. We cannot be one by sitting down to have a discussion. Be assured, the more we discuss, the more divided we will be. We should never talk about mere doctrines. We must simply fellowship about Jesus and be perfected with the indwelling Christ.

Some may want to talk about whether baptism should be by immersion or sprinkling, by hot water or cold water, in fresh water or salt water, in lake water, river water, or in a swimming pool. However, it is best not to talk about these things. Some may want to talk about the Lord's table, asking, "What kind of bread should we have? Should it be leavened or unleavened? Should it be cut into pieces or should it be whole? Should there be many small cups or one big cup?" Again, it is best not to talk about these things. If we talk about this, we may fight with each other. Let us forget about the opinions and be perfected into one by Christ.

ONENESS BY CARING ONLY FOR CHRIST
IN 1 CORINTHIANS

Caring for Christ, Not Knowledge or Gifts

The Corinthian believers were rich in all utterance and in all knowledge, and they did not lack any gift (1 Cor. 1:5-7). In other words, they had all the utterance, they had all the knowledge, and they had all the gifts. On the one hand, this is wonderful, but on the other hand, they were divided by the knowledge and gifts (v. 10). They were divided because they were too much in the teachings and the gifts. Because they appreciated knowledge and gifts, some admired Paul, others appreciated Apollos, and still others treasured Cephas. They appreciated these brothers according to their gifts. Eventually, some said that they were of Paul, of Apollos, and of Cephas. The Corinthians were divided by knowledge and gifts. If someone is for knowledge and gifts, eventually he may appreciate one brother and belittle another. Then there will be division. We do not care for mere knowledge, Bible doctrines, or gifts. We care only for Christ.

If we care only for Christ, we can never say I am of Paul, I am of Cephas, or I am of Apollos. People today like to use the suffix -*ite*. Someone who follows Cephas, for example, is a "Cephasite." People take such names because they are too much for teachings and gifts. We should not be for teachings or for gifts. We should be only for Christ.

Being Attuned in the Same Mind and in the Same Opinion

In 1 Corinthians 1:10 Paul says, "Now I beseech you, brothers, through the name of our Lord Jesus Christ, that you all speak the same thing and that there be no divisions among you, but that you be attuned in the same mind and in the same opinion." How can we be attuned to the same mind? In verse 13 Paul asks, "Is Christ divided?" The way to be attuned is in Christ. The Jews require a sign, which is related to gifts, and the Greeks seek after wisdom, which is related to knowledge; but we preach Christ and Christ crucified. To us, the called ones, Christ is God's power and God's wisdom (1 Cor. 1:24).

We all need to be attuned by Christ. If we care for something other than Christ, we can never be attuned, and to be sure, we will be divided. We have to be attuned by Christ and with Christ. In 1 Corinthians 2:2 Paul says, "For I did not determine to know anything among you except Jesus Christ, and this One crucified." Paul seemed to say, "I came to you without a determination to know anything except Christ. Why must you Corinthians know so many other things? You have to be attuned by Christ and with Christ. You have to give up all the teachings, you have to give up all the gifts, and you have to give up all your opinions."

Some may be offended by my word. They may ask, "What kind of preacher is this? He tells us to drop all the teachings. We have spent many years to learn all the doctrines. Now this man is telling us to drop them." I would ask such ones to read 1 Corinthians again and again. In chapter one Paul said that the Corinthians had all utterance, all knowledge, and all the gifts (vv. 5-7), but in chapter three he said that they were still infants in Christ. He said that they were still childish, fleshly, and even fleshy (vv. 1-3). Their need was to be attuned by Christ and to grow. This is today's situation in Christianity.

There are many doctrines and gifts, but most Christians are divided by them.

Recovering the Genuine Oneness by Dropping Everything Other Than Christ

The Lord's recovery today is the recovery of the genuine oneness, the oneness of Christ. The Lord is going to recover us out of the teachings, out of the gifts, and out of the opinions back to Himself. In Christ we have oneness. Hallelujah for Christ! Do not talk to me about the gifts, teachings, or mere opinions, and do not ask me for my opinion. I have only one opinion, that is Christ. To only care for Christ is the way to be one.

How can we keep the oneness? It is by dropping the doctrines and giving up the gifts. If you have the gift of healing, would you give it up? We have to give it up. Otherwise, the gift of healing will become a dividing factor. This does not mean that we never use the gift of healing. Sometimes, we may use it, but we are not for the gift; we are only for Christ.

Sometimes people have come to argue with me about particular matters, but I have no desire to argue. If someone asks me whether or not we should have tambourines in the meetings, I have no opinion. If the sisters like to play the tambourine, they can play many tambourines at once and I will not be bothered. Some saints, however, may be so bothered that they cannot come to a meeting with tambourines. If this is the case, they are right away divided. Let me ask you, "To what kind of meeting would you go?" Perhaps, you may need to take a "church tour," traveling through so many so-called churches in order to find a place that fits your taste. However, if it is suitable to your taste, it may not be suitable to others' taste, so eventually we all become divided. How can we keep the oneness in this way?

The Lord today is recovering the oneness. All the divisions are a shame to the Lord Jesus, and they are a real boast to the enemy. But if we today care for the oneness, this is a shame to the enemy. Even if we have only a small number, we still can boast to the enemy, saying, "Satan, look at us. We have all come out of every kind of background. Now we are truly one.

Satan, you caused people to say that there is no possibility for Christians to be one. But now here we are; we are one." Right away Satan will be put to shame and will be cast out. The oneness is a real shame to Satan. We can boast, "Satan, we are one. We do not have natural friendship; rather, we are one in Christ, by Christ, with Christ, and for Christ."

We need to be attuned by Christ and with Christ, not caring for anything else. Forty years ago, if I saw guitar playing in a meeting, I would have done my best to stop it. Recently in New Zealand, however, I was in a meeting with fewer than sixty people but many guitars, and in addition to the guitars there were also tambourines. I was happy with all the instruments. In that meeting nothing bothered us. We were all one.

THE ONENESS OF THE SPIRIT IN EPHESIANS

Ephesians 4:3 says, "Being diligent to keep the oneness of the Spirit in the uniting bond of peace." The oneness of the Spirit is the Spirit Himself. The Spirit Himself is our oneness. We should care not for doctrines or for gifts but for the Spirit. The book of Ephesians does not emphasize doctrines or gifts because, as Paul says, they are childish things (v. 14). Rather, we all have to know Christ and His Body and care for the oneness of the Spirit. The real oneness is one Body, one Spirit, one hope, one Lord, one faith, one baptism, and one God (vv. 4-6). Do not care for the teachings, and do not care for the gifts. Only care for the oneness. Today under the confusion of Christianity, it is not easy for us to be one. We need the Lord's grace to be emancipated from every kind of division.

THE GROUND OF LOCALITY
BEING FOR ONENESS NOT FOR DIVISION

I regret to say that some of the saints who have read our publications concerning the ground of locality have used them to cause division. Some have said that they are taking the ground of locality in a certain city and that they do not want to have fellowship with others. This is a true division. The ground of locality is for oneness, not for division. If we take the ground of locality as a standing to be independent from other believers, we are divisive.

The Lord Jesus has only one flock in the whole universe and on the whole earth. Regardless of how many local churches there are, there is still one flock. The brothers in Akron are the local church there, but they should not say that they have nothing to do with the church in Chicago. If they say this, they lose the character of oneness, and they become a local sect. There are many local churches on this earth, yet they all are still one flock. Nothing can divide us. Even geography cannot divide us. Due to distance, of course, the saints meeting in Chicago as the church in Chicago cannot meet day by day with the church in Los Angeles. We are separated by geography, but we are not divided. We are still one flock.

Concerning the ground of locality, some in a certain locality told me, "We are the local church here, so we will build up something uniquely local. Look at a finger. Doesn't it have its own distinction?" In response I said, "Yes, it does have its distinction, but do not forget that the circulation of the blood is one in all the fingers. You may have a distinction in your place, but the fellowship must be one. For a finger to keep its distinction by cutting itself off from the circulation causes isolation and death. This kind of meeting is a sect. We are all distinctive enough naturally. There is no need for us to build up our distinction. Rather, we have to tear down all the distinctions." We must try our best to have fellowship among all the local churches. This is not to be organized, however. To be organized is wrong.

EXERCISING TO FELLOWSHIP
AMONG THE LOCAL CHURCHES FOR MUTUAL HELP

Today all the local churches in the United States can testify that they have received help from the church in Los Angeles, and the church in Los Angeles has also received help from the other churches. Today we practice "pray-singing" by praying over the lines of a hymn after we sing it. This did not start in Los Angeles. Los Angeles learned this from another locality. Similarly, pray-reading did not begin in Los Angeles. Los Angeles learned pray-reading from others. Do not think that the church in Los Angeles demands that others always learn from it. All the local churches in the United States can testify that Los Angeles never exercises any control over the other churches. Still, many can testify that whoever goes to have contact with the church in Los Angeles receives some help.

We all have to learn not to take an excuse and say, "We take the ground of locality. We are the church in a certain place, and we have nothing to do with others." If we say this, we become a local sect. One local church is not the flock. It is only a part of the unique flock. All the churches are one flock with one Shepherd. For us to be organized into one with a "head church" controlling the other churches is truly devilish. Rather, we need to realize that all the local churches are one flock, one Body. All the churches have to go on by following one another.

After a period of time the church in Chicago may have something new. This would be wonderful. Through fellowship the other churches may learn of it and get the benefit. Then the church in Akron may have something better, and through fellowship the local churches can again receive the benefit. A church should not say that it has made an official decision to follow Los Angeles, nor should it say that it has made the decision not to follow Los Angeles. Both are wrong. As long as we make a decision in an organizational way, both to follow or not to follow are wrong. For a hand to say that it has made the decision to follow or not to follow the feet is foolish. There is no need to do this. As long as a hand is in the body, there is no need for it to say anything. It should simply be in the body. Oh, the subtlety of the enemy! Do not talk about following or not following. Simply be in the Body. Simply take care of the indwelling Christ. Be attuned by Him and with Him, and do not care about anything else. Then we will all be one.

PRACTICING THE ONENESS
WITHOUT ANY ELEMENT OF DIVISION

There may be only ten believers living in one city, ten living in a nearby city, and ten more living in another. If all three cities are close to one another, they can all come together to meet. There is no need to be legal. Some may say that they need to take the ground of locality. The ten in one city should be the church in that city, and the ten in the other cities should be the churches in those cities. This is mere legality, and it may also be an excuse to make a division. Some may not like to be with certain others, so they may use this excuse to meet by themselves.

Do not forget that the ground of locality is for oneness. By fellowshipping together, the thirty saints who live in the three nearby cities may feel that they are too small and need to come together as one expression for the sake of the impact. This is absolutely right. Then, when they grow from thirty to two hundred, the Lord may lead them to be three separate local expressions in the three cities. That is also right, because they will still be one. Whether we all come together or we stay in three cities as separate expressions, we are still one. There is no division or element of division. We all are one flock.

Today in His recovery the Lord is going to recover the genuine oneness. It is a shame to the Lord that His people are divided into many sects. Now if some of His dear saints will come together, be liberated and be emancipated out of all kinds of divisions, this will be a real glory and boast for the Lord, from now until the end of this age.

CHAPTER FOURTEEN

THE ONENESS OF THE FAITH
AND THE WINDS OF TEACHING

Scripture Reading: Eph. 4:13-14; Rev. 2:2-4, 14-15, 20, 7, 17; 3:20

Ephesians 4:13-14 says, "Until we all arrive at the oneness of the faith and of the full knowledge of the Son of God, at a full-grown man, at the measure of the stature of the fullness of Christ, that we may be no longer little children tossed by waves and carried about by every wind of teaching in the sleight of men, in craftiness with a view to a system of error." Recently I was invited to a certain locality. On the first day I arrived, some older ones came to me, saying, "You have to do something to help us. Our young people are a problem. You don't know how loud they are! We older saints cannot bear that." After not too long, the younger ones also came and said, "You have to do something to help us. The older ones are so dead. We cannot tolerate them. Today the young people are so active, and we cannot be with those dead ones." I was in a real dilemma. Both the old ones and the young ones put pressure on me. Sometimes in our meetings we are active outwardly, and some pious, godly people cannot bear this. However, being loud or quiet is not a part of our faith. Rather, this is a matter of particular teachings.

There has been much disputation and fighting among believers concerning the Lord's table. We have spoken with different kinds of believers concerning this matter. Some say that using a single, large cup is not healthy and passes germs to everyone. However, if we change to using many little cups, people may say, "Doesn't the Bible speak of one cup? There is only one Body, not many." In the Lord's table meeting should we use unleavened bread or leavened bread? Some say it must be leavened because the church today is not pure. In Matthew 13:33 the three measures of meal were leavened, typifying the situation in Christianity, so some say it is scriptural to use leaven. Still, some say the bread must be unleavened. First Corinthians 5:8 says, "So then let us keep the feast, not with old leaven, neither with the leaven of malice and evil, but with the unleavened bread of sincerity and truth." Unleavened bread is also scriptural. Some would also ask what we use in the cup: juice or wine? The Lord Jesus spoke of neither juice or wine, but the "product of the vine" (Matt. 26:29). This really puzzles people. Some people also argue about which day to have the Lord's table. They say, "Every day is the Lord's Day. Acts 2 says that the disciples broke bread from house to house day by day" (v. 46). Others question if the Lord's table should be in the morning or in the evening. Some say that since the Lord's table is a supper, not a breakfast or a lunch, we cannot have it in the morning. There are many such arguments. I cannot tell how many different opinions we have faced in the past forty years. These things are not items of the faith.

THE FAITH

The faith is the items in which we believe. Because we believe these items, we are one with the Lord. If we do not believe them, we are separate from the Lord and are lost. Our faith consists of the Bible, God, the person and work of Christ, and the church. Christ was incarnated to be a man, and He lived on this earth for thirty-three and a half years. He went to the cross and died there, not merely due to persecution and not for martyrdom but for our redemption. Moreover, He was resurrected on the third day, He ascended to the heavens, and He is still there. He will come back as our Lord, our Bridegroom, and our King. This is the work of Christ. We must believe in this.

Moreover, Ephesians 4:3-4a says, "Being diligent to keep the oneness of the Spirit in the uniting bond of peace: one Body and one Spirit." We must also believe that the church is the unique Body of Christ. It is unique universally, and it is also unique locally. The Bible, God, the person and work of Christ, and the church are the unique items we must believe in. About these there should not be any argument. These are not winds of teachings. Everything other than these, whether or not it is scriptural and sound, belongs to the winds of teachings.

THE ONENESS OF THE FAITH

We Christians can never be one in doctrines. Whether or not we will be one in doctrines in the New Jerusalem, there is no possibility in this age for us all to be one in doctrine. If I were to raise a question about doctrine, even a husband and wife will have differences. A husband may agree with head covering, but his wife may not. After a meeting, they may go home to fight about it. We can never be one in doctrines, at least not in this age. However, we all need to be one in the faith, and we can be one.

We may illustrate the oneness of the faith with three brothers who are saved in the same summer through the preaching of the gospel. These three are joyful with the Lord's salvation. Soon afterward one goes to study at a Southern Baptist university, one goes to a Presbyterian college, and the third studies at an evangelical Bible institute. After one year's time they all return home. From the first day they arrive, they begin to fight. The first one picked up something from the Southern Baptists, the second picked up something different from the Presbyterians, and the third one picked up something else from the Bible institute. What they picked up was in addition to their faith. In that first summer, they all received the faith. They all believed that the Bible is God's Word, that God is triune, that He is our Father, that Christ is the Son of God as well as the Son of Man becoming our Redeemer, and that Christ has a Body, the church. This was wonderful, but afterward they went to different schools, picked up different kinds of doctrines, and came home again not only with Christ and the faith, but with so many other things. Now they fight one against the other. This is because they all are children. All children like toys, and all the different doctrines are toys. Therefore, Paul said that we all have to grow; we all have to go on until we all arrive at the oneness of the faith (4:13).

In the ancient times there were Jewish believers and Greek believers, and they all received the same faith. However, many Jewish believers still kept their Judaistic concept, and many Greek believers kept certain kinds of Greek philosophy. If they would remain Christian children, they would fight with one another, but if they would grow and go on to be perfected, they would all arrive at the oneness of the faith which they had received at the beginning.

In the local churches we help people to grow. Firstly, we help people to call, "O Lord!" Then we help them to pray-read: "Amen! In the beginning was the Word. And the Word was God. Hallelujah! Praise the Lord! Jesus is Lord!" Then they throw out all the things they picked up. Nothing is left but Jesus. They can declare, "Jesus is my food. Jesus is my life. Jesus is my enjoyment. Jesus is everything." If we all grow with the help of the local churches, all the things we have picked up eventually will go away, and we will arrive at the oneness of the faith. We will be "no longer little children tossed by waves and carried about by every wind of teaching" (v. 14).

CONTENDING FOR THE FAITH AND
KEEPING THE FAITH

Jude 3 says to "earnestly contend for the faith." It does not say to contend for the doctrines. When I was a young Christian, I was taught to contend for doctrines. I was baptized by sprinkling when I was a teenager. After I was saved, I was adjusted to be baptized by immersion. I was taught to contend for immersion, and I did it. I fought nearly every day for immersion. After a long time, however, I came to know that contending in this way is foolish. The Bible never tells us to contend for the doctrine but to contend for the faith.

First Timothy 6:12 says, "Fight the good fight of the faith." At the end of his course Paul said, "I have fought the good fight;...I have kept the faith" (2 Tim. 4:7). Paul said that he kept the faith, not the doctrine. In the New Testament the word *faith* has two meanings. First it refers to our believing action or ability. It is the action or ability to believe in the Bible, in God, and in Christ. This is our faith, the subjective faith. Faith also has another meaning, referring to the things in which we believe. This is the objective faith. When we speak of the oneness of the faith, faith is objective, the things in which we believe, not the believing action, the believing ability. We have to fight for this faith. If anyone would say, as the modernists do, that Christ is only a man and not the Son of God, I would never shake hands with him. He is one of the antichrists (1 John 4:3; 2 John 10-11). I would never recognize such a one as my brother. By the Lord's grace and mercy, however, I do not care whether someone is for baptism by sprinkling or by immersion. As long as he believes, as long as he has this faith, he is my brother.

OUR SPECIALITY AND GENERALITY

We believe in the Bible, in God, in Christ, and in His redemptive work, and we also recognize that the church is uniquely one in this universe and in any locality. As to other teachings, we may or may not take them. This is up to the Lord's leading. Whether we have a noisy meeting or a quiet meeting is up to the situation. If the saints are quiet, let them be quiet. If the saints are noisy and some like to play the tambourine, we have to say, "Praise the Lord!" It depends on the situation. In other words, it is up to the Lord's leading. We all have to be in our spirit. Then we are one.

We can say this based on Romans 14. Paul was a great teacher. As such a one he knew that since this is the day of grace, all things are good for eating (1 Tim. 4:3-4). However, in Romans 14 he gave a very liberal and neutral word: "He who eats, let him not despise him who does not eat; and he who does not eat, let him not judge him who eats, for God has received him....He who regards that day, regards it to the Lord; and he who eats, eats to the Lord, for he gives thanks to God; and he who does not eat, does not eat to the Lord, and he gives thanks to God" (vv. 3, 6). How neutral and liberal he was! Did Paul not know that in the age of grace there is no need to regard a certain day? All days are the same. Paul knew this better than we do, but in this chapter he did not teach such a thing. Instead, he took a neutral stand. This was because of what he had said in chapter twelve concerning the Body life. Today many Christians talk about the Body life according to Romans 12, but they neglect chapter fourteen. Without chapter fourteen we could never have the Body life. We need chapter fourteen to keep the Body life in chapter twelve.

We have to be neutral, general, and liberal. Of course, I do not mean liberal like today's modernists. As to the faith we would never be general; we would be specific. We are specific as to the Bible, God our Father, our Lord Jesus Christ, His Person, His incarnation, crucifixion, resurrection, ascension, and coming back, and as to the church being one. We would never tolerate anything against the truth. These items are our speciality. Concerning other things, however, we must be general. This is our generality. Baptism by immersion and by sprinkling are both all right. Both bare feet and covered feet in the meetings are all right. Using wine or grape juice in the Lord's table is all right, and using either a big cup or a small cup is also all right. If you would take the Lord's table in the morning, that is all right, and if you would take it at midnight, that is also all right. We are liberal in all the generalities, but we are special in our speciality. In our speciality we would not give any ground. We would not give in. We would pay the price of our life for the faith. Brothers and sisters, can we all say this? Can we put this into practice? If so, then we can keep the oneness of the faith.

THE CAUSE OF THE DEGRADATION OF THE CHURCH

Leaving the First Love for the Lord

From chapters two and three of Revelation we can see that the degradation of the churches in the ancient time was first due to the leaving of their first love to the Lord (Rev. 2:4). They left their first love because they cared for the work; they labored, working and doing things for others. They were even very fundamental, very sound. They would not take anything that was evil, and they tried anyone pretending to be an apostle (v. 2). They were so fundamental, so sound, and so scriptural, yet they left their love for the Lord. The Lord does not care for any work. The Lord only cares for Himself. If we would allow something else, even the best things for the Lord, to come in to take the place of the Lord, we are wrong. This is like a wife's relationship with her husband. Regardless of how much she does for her husband, if something comes in to take his place in her heart, she is wrong. Leaving the first love, or the best love, toward the Lord was the cause of the church's degradation.

The Lord told the church in Ephesus that they needed to overcome (v. 7). In the past we had a wrong concept. We thought that to overcome was simply to overcome our little temper or our little besetting sin. In the book of Revelation to overcome does not mean this. It means to overcome the degraded Christianity, to overcome the present situation of Christianity in its leaving of the best, the first, love to the Lord. Many in Christianity take care of the work in the mission field, in Bible studies, and in helping others, but they do not care for the Lord. Dr. A. W. Tozer published an article saying that if Christian leaders were holding a conference to discuss how to work for Christ, and Christ walked in, they would not recognize Him. This indicates that in today's Christianity the Lord Jesus has no place. Much work fully preoccupies today's Christianity.

The Lord Jesus promised, "To him who overcomes, to him I will give to eat of the tree of life, which is in the Paradise of God" (v. 7). We need not work so much; rather, we have to eat. Eating was God's original concept, even in the garden of Eden. At the very beginning of the Bible, God was concerned for our eating (Gen. 2:9, 16-17). It is as if He said, "Don't work for Me. You have to eat Me. Eat the tree of life." Eventually the Lord Jesus came. The Jewish people thought He was a great man, and they tried to make him a king, but the Lord Jesus withdrew from them (John 6:15). The next day He came back and told them, "I am the bread of life" (v. 48). By this He meant, "Don't make Me that big. I don't like to be that big. I like to be eaten by you. He who eats Me, he also shall live because of Me. I am the bread of life. I am just good for eating. I don't care for what you do. I care for what you eat. Eat Me."

The Lord's recovery is to bring us back to the beginning (Matt. 19:8). We must go back to eating. Do not do so much work. Rather, take care of Christ. Take care of the enjoyment of Christ. Christ does not care much for the work we do for Him. He mainly cares how much we gain Him, enjoy Him, and take Him in, that is, how much we eat Him. "To him who overcomes, to him I will give to eat of the tree of life, which is in the Paradise of God" (Rev. 2:7). Eating truly brings us back to the beginning. This is the reality of the Lord's recovery.

The Teaching of Balaam
and the Teaching of the Nicolaitans

Following the church in Ephesus, the other churches became more and more degraded by taking doctrines, such as the teaching of Balaam and the teaching of the Nicolaitans (Rev. 2:14-15). If today we are still for certain doctrines, sooner or later all the other doctrines will creep in. Because Christians were for doctrines, there was the ground for the doctrine of Balaam to creep in. If they had not been for doctrines, they would have said, "No, we don't care for this doctrine. There is no room, no entry, for any doctrines to creep in." Today's Christianity is too much for doctrines. Too many there have itching ears, heaping up to themselves teachers (2 Tim. 4:3). Some prefer to have a famous theological doctor or missionary come to speak to them. When there is a good speaker, the church buildings are crowded, but when the prayer meeting comes, only a few persons attend. Sometimes only the pastor, his wife, and the janitor attend the prayer meeting. The Lord said, "But I have a few things against you, that you have some there who hold the teaching of Balaam" (Rev. 2:14). Among so many doctrines, the doctrine of Balaam and the doctrine of the Nicolaitans crept into the church in Pergamos.

The Teaching of Jezebel

To the church in Thyatira the Lord Jesus said, "But I have something against you, that you tolerate the woman Jezebel, she who calls herself a prophetess and teaches and leads My slaves astray to commit fornication and to eat idol sacrifices"

(v. 20). The evil woman Jezebel was prophesied by the Lord Jesus in Matthew 13:33. The Lord Jesus sowed Himself as a seed which grew into wheat (vv. 3, 24). Out of the grains of wheat comes the meal for making a loaf (v. 33). The evil woman, signifying the Roman Catholic Church, not only mixed but hid leaven, signifying the evil things, the corrupting factor, in the meal. The Roman Catholic Church took many hidden, pagan things as the corrupting factor and hid all these things under the covering of Christ. It presents Christ to people, but something is hidden under the covering of Christ. In a hidden way it corrupts, damages, and ruins people, yet they have no consciousness of it. The Lord Jesus hates such teachings. Therefore, we must learn not to take mere teachings. Do not be offended by this word. If you still intend to take mere teachings, you will become leavened, if not today, then eventually.

To grow into the wheat to produce the meal in Matthew 13 requires transformation. In two of the last parables in Matthew 13 there are the treasure hidden in the field and the pearl of great value (vv. 44-46). The treasure in the field must be either gold, precious stones, or pearls. These things can never be leavened. We all have to go on to have the growth and to have transformation. When we are the fine meal, the fine flour, it is easy for us to be leavened, but if we all are transformed into precious stones and pearls, no one can leaven us. We do not care for mere teachings.

OVERCOMING THE TEACHINGS AND EATING JESUS AS THE TREE OF LIFE, THE HIDDEN MANNA, AND THE FEAST

The Lord Jesus promised those who overcome to eat of the tree of life, the hidden manna, and the feast (Rev. 2:7, 17; 3:20). He said, "Behold, I stand at the door and knock; if anyone hears My voice and opens the door, then I will come in to him and dine with him and he with Me" (3:20). In Revelation 2 and 3 there are three categories of eating: eating of the tree of life, eating the hidden manna, and feasting. In the garden of Eden there was the tree of life to be eaten (Gen. 2:9, 16). In the wilderness the children of Israel ate of the manna (Exo. 16:14-15), and when they came into the good land, they held the feasts (Lev. 23). Today we are in the fulfillment of the tree of life, the manna, and the feasts.

We need to overcome the present situation of degraded Christianity, and to overcome means to overcome all the teachings, the different concepts, and the different opinions and come back to Jesus, not merely to understand Him but to eat Him as the tree of life, the hidden manna, and our feast. Eating is the main thing we practice in the local churches. In the local churches we do not care for the teachings or doctrines. We only care for the eating of Jesus, the enjoyment of Jesus. Here we are one. In the eating we have no opinions, so we are one. If we are for doctrines, we surely will have opinions; we will be divided. May the Lord be merciful to us. Here we have the real recovery. The real recovery is to overcome the present situation of today's Christianity, that is, to give up all the doctrines and simply come back to the spirit, taking Christ as the unique nourishing factor to enjoy Him. This is the recovery of the church. The church life is a life of the enjoyment of Christ. I do hope that we all will see this.

Chapter Fifteen

THE RECOVERY OF GOD'S BUILDING

(1)

Scripture Reading: 1 Cor. 3:6, 9b, 12; 1 Pet. 2:2-5; Eph. 2:21-22; 4:11-16; Col. 2:19; Rom. 12:2, 5

GOD'S WORK OF CREATION AND BUILDING

As we have seen, the two ends of the Bible reflect each other. What is there at the beginning is also there at the end. At the beginning of the Bible there was the tree of life, and at the end of the Bible we have the same tree of life. At the beginning there was the river flowing, and at the end the flowing river again appears. At the beginning of the Bible there were gold, bdellium (pearl), and onyx, the precious stones in the flow of the flowing river. At the end of the Bible there are the same materials: gold, pearl, and precious stones built together as a city. Lastly, at the beginning of the Bible there was a bride built up by God, and at the end of the Bible there is also a bride.

We must be clear that at the beginning there was not a city; there was just a garden. At the end of the Bible, however, instead of a garden there is a city. The record at the two ends of the Bible is figurative. As a figure, a garden mostly signifies something natural; in a garden there are the things of nature. In a city, however, the main feature is building. In the whole universe, according to the record of the Bible, God has only two kinds of works: the work of creation and the work of building. His first work was the work of creation, and His second work is the work of building. Moreover, God's creation is for God's building. However, many Christians have not seen this important point.

There is no doubt that God's creation has been fully completed. Now God's work is the building. Genesis, the first book of the Bible, is a book of creation, and Revelation, the last book of the Bible, is a book of building. The Bible began with creation, and it ends with God's building. Now God is in the process of building, and we are under the process of God's building. This is why in these last days the Lord will recover the important matter of His building.

THE RECOVERY OF GOD'S
ULTIMATE AND CONSUMMATE INTENTION

With the Reformation about five hundred years ago, God began His recovery. Throughout these five hundred years many things have been recovered. The first item recovered was justification by faith. Following that many other items were recovered. We believe that the last item of God's recovery is the building, because this is the last item, the last point, in the whole Bible. What is the last item in the entire Bible of sixty-six books? It is a city built by God with gold, pearl, and precious stones.

Without a doubt history shows us that this point has been fully neglected. Even today many dear saints pay their full attention to the preaching of the gospel, the edification of the saints, holiness, the victorious life, spirituality, and to many other things. Many dear Christians are busy with many things, but very few today care for the building. People today spend much time for the preaching of the gospel, and nothing is wrong with this. We do need the preaching of the gospel, but we need to realize that preaching is not for its own sake. Many are also busy with the study of the Bible. That is not wrong; it is absolutely right to study the Bible, but study should not be merely for the sake of study. Today we also have mission work. That is marvelous, and we praise the Lord for this. In the past few centuries the Lord raised up much mission work to bring His gospel to every corner of this earth. However, mission work should not be merely for mission work. The Lord also raised up the experience of the inner life, especially in the past three hundred years. Since the time of Madame Guyon, this has been a great help to many seeking saints, and we again thank the Lord for this. However, even the inner life should not be for the inner life. Many doctrines have also been recovered. We thank God for this, but even the doctrines should not be only for the doctrines. We also have the so-called Pentecostal or charismatic things. Of course, some are not genuine; some are no doubt human-manufactured, but still some are real. We praise the Lord for all these items, yet all these items should not be for their own sake. They should be for the building. God's intention is ultimately to have the building.

The building is God's ultimate consummation. Read the Bible again. If we do not have the building of God, we are short of at least the last two chapters. Our book of Revelation may only have twenty chapters. It may not have chapters twenty-one and twenty-two. We very much need these two chapters. In these last days the Lord has truly come to these two chapters.

THE BUILDING AS THE ULTIMATE CONSUMMATION IN ROMANS

The building is the ultimate consummation not only in the entire Bible but also in all the Epistles, including those written by Paul, Peter, and John. In all the Epistles the ultimate point is the building. Romans, for example, is a sketch, an outline, with a good sequence of the Christian life and the church life. In the first chapters of Romans there is a picture, a record, of sinners. Following this, there is the revelation of how these awful sinners can be justified. In chapters three, four, and the first half of five, sinners have justification by faith through the blood of Christ. Then Romans shows us that regardless of how much we are justified through the blood of Christ, we were born in Adam, so we still have the old nature, but by God's grace we have been transferred out of Adam into Christ. In Adam we have the flesh, but with Christ we have the spirit. Now there is no need for us to remain in the flesh; rather, we need to walk in the spirit. In the spirit we have full salvation in life, including the liberation from besetting sins.

In the spirit we enjoy all the riches of God's salvation in
Christ. This is wonderful, but we should not stop at the spirit
in Romans 8. We need to go on, passing through chapters
nine, ten, and eleven until we arrive at chapter twelve. What
we have in chapter twelve is the building, the Body (vv. 4-5).
Without the building, that is, without the Body, we simply do
not have the conclusion of this book.

Romans concludes with the Body, the building. However,
many Christians today talk about the Body merely in a doctrinal way, a way that is not practical. I would like to ask,
"Where is the Body for you?" Do not merely say that the Lord
has a Body in the universe. Practically speaking, where is the
Body? As the members of the Body we must be practical, but
regrettably, very few Christians are in the Body life practically. The Body is merely doctrinal and objective. We cannot
say where the Body is for them; perhaps it is in the air.
According to the revelation of all the Epistles, however, the
Body must be very present, instant, and practical to us. We
need to be in the Body practically, instantly, and presently, not
"in the air" or in the "by and by." We must have the Body
today.

BEING FITTED AND BUILT TOGETHER IN EPHESIANS

Romans is an outline, but in an outline we do not have the
details. Therefore, from Romans we must go on to pass
through 1 and 2 Corinthians and Galatians until we arrive at
Ephesians. Many Christians today love the book of Ephesians
because they realize that it is a book on the church. However,
it is regrettable that many Christians take this book of the
church merely in a doctrinal way, making the church only a
doctrine.

Practically speaking again, "Where is the church for you?"
Some may say that there are many churches. Yes, there are
many so-called churches and all kinds of "churches." In every
big city today without exception there are many "churches,"
but where is the church for you? If we say that the Presbyterian Church or the Methodist Church is our church, can we
truly agree with what we say? Do we truly consider that the
Presbyterian Church is the genuine church? If we would all be

honest, we will admit that while we are saying yes, deep within us something is saying no. We can fool many people, and we can even be cheated by our own mind, but something within us is sincere; that is our regenerated human spirit. The spirit within us often causes us to have a sensation of dissatisfaction about this matter. People today talk about the church mostly in a doctrinal way, but in actuality they do not have the church. They may have a denomination, a group of Christians, a sect, or whatever they call it, but deep within they realize that this is not the genuine church.

Ephesians is not merely doctrinal; it is very practical. Verse 21 of chapter two says, "In whom all the building, being fitted together, is growing into a holy temple in the Lord." To speak of all the building being fitted together may sound doctrinal, but following this verse is verse 22, which says, "In whom you also are being built together into a dwelling place of God in spirit." When I was young, I was bothered by this verse. I thought it was not necessary because the idea of the building was completed in verse 21. After saying that in Christ all the building, being fitted together, is growing into a holy temple in the Lord, there seems to be no need to say anything further, but verse 21 goes on to say, "In whom you also." We should underline the two words *you also*. Who are the you? It is we as a local church. All the building includes all the Christians, but *you also* refers to the local saints at Ephesus. This is very practical. Verse 21 may be doctrinal, but we can never consider verse 22 to be doctrinal. You also, the local saints in the place where you are, are being built together.

We are being built together into a dwelling place of God in spirit. According to the context, *spirit* should have a small *s*. It does not refer directly to a building in the Holy Spirit; the dwelling place of God in the church today is in our spirit. The building of the local church is in our spirit. This also is very practical.

If we go on from chapter two, we can see that chapter four is even more practical. Verses 11 to 13 say, "And He Himself gave some as apostles and some as prophets and some as evangelists and some as shepherds and teachers, for the perfecting of the saints unto the work of the ministry, unto the building up of the Body of Christ, until we all arrive at the oneness of the faith and of the full knowledge of the Son of God, at a full-grown man, at the measure of the stature of the fullness of Christ." The church is a collective, corporate entity, the new man. The new man is not an individual man but a corporate one, so the church must arrive at a full-grown man.

Verse 14 continues, "That we may be no longer little children tossed by waves and carried about by every wind of teaching in the sleight of men, in craftiness with a view to a system of error." This verse speaks of every wind of teaching, not wind of heresy. We should not think that only heresy is a wind to blow us away. Many sound, fundamental, good, and genuine doctrines are also winds to blow us away from the Body and from the Head. Throughout all the centuries the enemy has subtly utilized doctrines to distract the seeking members from the Body life and from the Head.

Verses 15 and 16 say, "But holding to truth in love, we may grow up into Him in all things, who is the Head, Christ." We grow not only in Christ but into Him. Verse 15 speaks of growing into Him, while verse 16 speaks of something out from Him. Verse 16 says, "Out from whom all the Body, being joined together and being knit together through every joint of the rich supply and through the operation in the measure of each one part, causes the growth of the Body unto the building up of itself in love." This verse does not speak of something doctrinal; it is very practical.

ALL THINGS BEING FOR THE BUILDING

The building is the ultimate point of all the Epistles written by the apostles. Regrettably, however, most of the seeking Christians today have not seen this. They care for many good things, but they simply do not care for this one matter. Some say that as long as they have soul-winning, bringing people to Christ, that is wonderful. Others say that as long as they teach the Bible, to know the Word of God, that is wonderful. Still others say that as long as they have a number of believers going out to the mission fields in foreign countries to spread the gospel to further the kingdom of God, that is wonderful. Some say that as long as they edify people and help them to grow in life, that is wonderful, while many today say that as long as they help people to speak in tongues and gain the charismatic gifts, that is wonderful. I also say that these things are wonderful.

However, if we speak with many believers about the building of the Body, they may say, "This is a hard matter. Do not talk about this. The Lord Himself will take care of this some day in the by and by." We should not speak in this way. We are for the gospel preaching, we are for the Bible, we are for the mission work, we are for the inner life, and we are for the proper, genuine charismatic things. However, we need to realize that all these are for the building. God is interested not merely in pieces of stone; His interest is in His house.

What do we have today? Is it a house or only a pile of materials? I would even ask those who meet as a local church: Are you piling up or building up? To pile up is one thing, but to be built up is another. We may pile together all the materials for a house, but it is still not a house. Many Christian free groups are just a pile, not the building. The Bible clearly says that in the building all the materials are fitted together (Eph. 2:21). This is not merely to pile up but to build up. It is easy to tell people where gospel preaching, campaigns, and crusades are. It is easy to say where home Bible studies are, and it is easy to say where mission work in many countries is. Likewise, it is easy to say where speaking in tongues is. However, where is the building today? Someone may have been a Christian for many years, and he may know many Christian things, but can he point out where the building is?

BEING GOOD ONLY FOR THE BUILDING

We may also ask, "With whom have we been built?" Someone may say that he has been related to the people in his mission or Bible study class, but that is only a kind of relationship; it is not the building. When that person feels happy, he will remain in that relationship, but when he feels unhappy, he will pull himself out of it. Can a stone in a building say, "Now I am unhappy; I am going to pull myself out of the building"? The Lord Jesus may say to a built-up believer,

"Little stone, I am sorry. You cannot pull yourself out. You have been built in."

Stones are just right for the building. They are useless for other purposes, but they are very useful for the purpose of building. I am a little man who has been wrecked by the Lord Jesus for the church life for forty years, and I have never regretted it. I cannot pull myself out of the building, and neither can any other built-up member.

NOT BEING "CHURCH TOURISTS" BUT BEING BUILT TOGETHER

Today it is difficult to find built-up believers. It is easy, however, to see many wandering Christians. They are "church tourists." Such a believer may say, "Three years ago I had a tour and some good sightseeing in the Southern Baptist Church, but after a short while I got fed up with that, so I traveled to the Presbyterian Church and had a tour there. At the beginning it was marvelous, but eventually I was disappointed. Then I found a 'tour guide,' and he brought me to some charismatic meetings. There I had some good sightseeing of speaking in tongues and holy rollers, holy jumpers, holy laughers, and holy weepers. Eventually, however, I was also fed up with that. Now I am wondering where I shall have my next tour." This is an illustration of today's situation. There are too many church tourists and church travelers. One month a brother may feel happy with a group because it fits his natural disposition and taste, but this kind of natural love cannot last long. After another three months he may become unhappy with that group. Then he will look in the church directory in the newspaper and go traveling again.

BUILDING THE CHURCH AS A SHAME TO SATAN

Concerning the building, we must not care for what people say. We must not care for human faces, the "faces of clay." What people say means nothing. Today others may give us a good report, but tomorrow they may give us an evil report. We praise the Lord for the good reports and for the evil reports. Whatever people say, let them say it. They are only "faces of clay."

Today the Lord's interest is to have a building. We should read the Bible again, particularly the Epistles in the New Testament. It is so clear that before the Lord's second coming, He must gain His building on this earth. If the Lord cannot accomplish this, this will be a great shame to Him. Satan will use this to challenge the Lord. He will say, "Jesus, look. For over two thousand years You have been trying to build up something, but You never did it. All the time I frustrated and damaged the building." Do you think that the Lord Jesus will tolerate this? In 1948 the Lord re-formed the nation of Israel. A large number of Arab countries surrounded this little nation and tried to make a conspiracy against her, but they could not win. Now the Lord Jesus can say, "Little Satan, are you ready? I have been tolerating you for twenty centuries. Have you seen what I did with Israel? Now is My time. Now I am going to gain My building on the earth."

I am so happy for the church in Los Angeles. The city of Los Angeles is famous throughout the world mainly for Hollywood. As the movie capital, it is the corruption-growing factor of the whole world. It is the darkest city on the earth, but the Lord Jesus can say, "Satan, have you seen? I have built up a church in the movie capital, even in your capital." I am not speaking these things in a light way. Be assured; wait and see. Here and there in the leading cities of the United States and of other countries the Lord Jesus will build up something. He will challenge Satan and say, "Satan, even in your territory I am building up something." For many centuries even Christians, the Lord's people, have said that it is impossible to have a proper church life in a visible way, that the church must be invisible. Now, however, the Lord Jesus will tell Satan, "I will build up something very practical and visible. It is absolutely possible. I will make some of My people one. I will shut up their opinions. I will tear down their doctrinal concepts about the church, and I will build up something of Myself by My life. What can you say, Satan? Are you ready?" The Lord will do this.

THE HOUSE OF GOD BEING GOD'S SATISFACTION

When many of us came into the church life, we became "crazy." Many of us can testify that we had been touring and sightseeing many places. None ever satisfied us until the day we came to the church, because immediately when we came in, the dispensing of Christ within us told us that we were home. About forty years ago, I was satisfied in this way. I was born and raised in formal Christianity. Later, I was with the Brethren for seven and a half years, and I received edification and the knowledge of fundamental Christianity. One day, however, I came into the church. I can never forget that; I was very excited. I have heard the young people in Los Angeles expressing this satisfaction with the following song:

> We have the local churches, local churches
>   down in our heart,
> Down in our heart, down in our heart.
> We have the local churches, local churches
>   down in our heart,
> Down in our heart to stay.
> And we're so happy, so very happy;
> We have the local churches in our heart.
> And we're so happy, so very happy;
> We have the local churches in our heart.

The reason we were satisfied when we found the church is that God was satisfied. When the naughty young Jacob ran away from home and was on the way to his uncle's house, he was a wanderer. However, Jacob never considered that God was also a wandering God. At that time Jacob had no home, but neither did God have a home. Therefore, a dream came to Jacob (Gen. 28:10-19). God seemed to be saying to him, "Jacob, this is My house. This is not only your dream; this is My dream. I have been dreaming, and I am still dreaming of a house on this earth."

Nothing is so precious as the house of God on this earth. When Ezekiel saw the house of God, the Lord said to him, "Son of Man, this is the place of My throne and the place of the soles of My feet" (43:7). Because we Christians were wrongly taught, we often dream of going to heaven. However, God is the opposite; He is always dreaming of coming to the earth. He is earth-sick. Eventually, the Lord will come, but before His coming back He must build up something. His building may not be on a large scale, but here and there in all the leading cities, on a smaller scale the Body will be fully built. The Body will be not piled up or simply gathered together, but built together. Then the Lord Jesus will say, "Satan, have you seen? What can you say? In this city I have built up something."

BUILDING THE CHURCH
BY COMING BACK TO THE PROPER GROUND

Today there are about thirteen million Jews on the earth. Of these thirteen million, however, only about two million have returned to Israel. All the thirteen million claim to be Jews, but only those two million who went back can say that they are the nation of Israel. It is not wrong for them to say this. No one can say to them, "Why do you call yourself the nation of Israel? You are sectarian for claiming this. The nation of Israel includes all the members of the race of Hebrews." Yes, it includes all members of the race of Hebrews, but most of them would not go back to Israel. Even the United Nations recognizes that only those who have returned are the nation of Israel.

Many dear friends have come to challenge me, asking, "Why do you call yourself the church in Los Angeles? Are we not also the church?" I have replied, "Thank God you are the church, but you are not at home. You are like the Jews who are in New York, not in Israel. You may be a 'Hebrew,' but you are in 'Japan, Germany, or France'; you are not in your fathers' land. As long as a Jew stays in New York, he should not and cannot blame those who say they are the nation of Israel. You cannot be the nation of Israel in New York. You must be the nation of Israel in the fathers' land. In the same way, do not argue about the church. Rather, if you want to be the church in Los Angeles, come back home."

No doubt, all the believers in Los Angeles are the members of the church in Los Angeles. Why then do they stay in the denominations? If they do not come back, that is their responsibility. They must not put the blame upon us. Therefore, if someone is a Jew today, I would advise him to go back to Israel at any cost. In the same principle, if someone is an honest Christian, I would advise him to come back to the church at any cost.

THE BUILDING BEING WITH THE RETURNING MINORITY, NOT WITH SPIRITUAL GIANTS

Under God's economy, all His people in the Old Testament were in the good land. Due to their degradation, however, some were carried away to Babylon in the east and to Egypt in the south. Were they not Hebrews? Every one of them was a Hebrew, but many of them were Hebrews in captivity, in Babylon. The people, the persons, were right, but the place was not right. After seventy years the Lord gave the commandment, and some, a minority, a small number, went back to Jerusalem. The spiritual giants such as Daniel remained in Babylon. Among the returned ones there were almost no spiritual giants. Instead, they were a mess. Some even married Gentile wives. Regardless of that, however, the rebuilding of the house of God on this earth was not with the spiritual giants in Babylon. The rebuilding of the temple was with the returning minority.

Regardless of how spiritual the Hebrews were, in the captivity they never had the Lord's glory. After the rebuilding of the temple in Jerusalem, however, the glory of Jehovah filled the temple. In addition, the first coming of the Lord Jesus to the earth was brought about not through those at Babylon but through the descendants of the returning ones. This is not a small matter. The Lord Jesus was supposed to be born of a descendant of David in Bethlehem. If in the ancient times there had been no return from the captivity, how could Christ have been born? It would have been impossible. Regardless of how good the spiritual giants in Babylon were, they were useless for the Lord's first coming. Only the little descendants of the returned captivity, like Mary and Joseph, were very prevailing to bring the Lord to this earth. We must care not only about our spirituality but about God's economy. Whether one is spiritual or not spiritual in Babylon makes little difference, but whether or not he returns makes a great difference. With the return there is the rebuilding of the temple. With the return there is the glory coming down to the earth. With the return there is the first coming of the Lord Jesus. This is not a matter of our spiritual situation or condition, of our personal spirituality. It is a matter of God's economy.

Today it is the same in principle. That is why I say that if someone is a Hebrew, he should do his best at any cost, to pay any price, to go back to Palestine to join the nation of Israel. This is a matter of God's economy. If one is an honest Christian, however, he must do his best to get into the church. There is no argument about this. If someone does not do this, he will "miss the boat." We cannot delay the Lord, but we may not be gained by the Lord. The Lord will still go on, but we may not "make the boat."

We do not care for a large scale; we care for the standard and the principle. We are not here for any movement. We are not here for gospel preaching, although we have it. We are not here for the inner life, although we have much of it. We are not here for Bible study, although we know the Bible very well. We are not here for any gift, although we have the gifts. What are we here for? We are here for the Lord's recovery. We are here for the building.

NOT CARING FOR THE REPROACH OF OPPOSERS

Please read Ezra, Nehemiah, Hosea, and Zechariah. Some people despised and reproached the rebuilding of Jerusalem, saying that what the returned ones were building was a small matter (Neh. 4:1-4). Is the building a small matter? Wait and see. The Lord does not care for spiritual giants; spiritual giants mean little to Him. The Lord will harvest all the wandering seekers. In the United States the crop is ripe, and the timing is right. This is the time for the Lord's harvest. The Lord will bring in the wanderers like a flock. He will satisfy every hungry, seeking saint by means of the local churches.

Although I am working hard all the time, every night I have a good sleep. I am so happy that the Lord's recovery is not a human doing. It is the Lord's doing today on the earth, and it is absolutely new. The Lord's care for His recovery can be illustrated by His care for the nation of Israel. Recently, after the Arab leaders conspired together in a conference, the

Lord looked at Nasser, the Egyptian leader, and seemed to say, "You are ready to go," and Nasser died. Even some secular newspapers said that the death of Nasser was a miracle. Since that time, there have been no great leaders among the Arab countries. Egypt gained military and economic skills from Russia, but recently Egypt cut off all its high officials who were in favor of Communism. Russia was puzzled over this, not knowing what to do. This also was the Lord's doing. The unity of the Arab countries has been broken, and little Israel is happy. Praise the Lord, the Arab countries cannot do anything with the little nation of Israel. In a similar way, the recovery of the church life is something of the Lord's doing, and it is marvelous in our eyes.

GAINING A BOAST FOR THE LORD
AND A SHAME TO THE ENEMY

Through our experiences, many can testify that when we are for the building in our church service, we are so happy. Nothing makes us as happy as being built together with others. Even to know the Bible does not make us very happy, but when we are coordinated in the church service, we are in the third heaven. This is a confirmation from the Lord. It is the indication of where He is and the sign of what He is after. The Lord is after His building.

This building is a shame to the enemy. The little Satan is shaking; he is trembling at the building. He is afraid of nothing else. He is not afraid to see people saved, but he is afraid of the building up of the saints. There is no need to speak of eighty to a hundred being built up; if only thirty to fifty are built up in a locality, this will shake Satan. Of course, as we have seen, we need growth and transformation for the building. Nothing muddy or natural is qualified for the Lord's work. Only the Lord Himself is qualified. All the materials for the building of the city of God must be gold, pearl, and precious stones. There must be nothing muddy or wooden. Therefore, we need transformation. Praise the Lord, we are under the process of the Lord's transformation!

I have been in the Lord's recovery for many years. I can tell you and the Lord can testify, I was very happy in the past because I saw the Lord's recovery, but I have never been as happy as I am now in the United States. To be here in the United States is like a dream. We never dreamed that we would be here, but here we are. Before I came to this country, certain ones spoke poorly to me about American Christians. This disappointed me very much. But now that I am here, I am not disappointed. Day by day I am encouraged from many directions. What I have seen is absolutely different from what I heard. What I heard was black, but what I now see is white. This is marvelous, and it is the Lord's doing. What is the Lord doing? He is doing the work of building. Preaching is for the building; the study of the Word is for the building; the inner life is for the building; the gifts are for the building; and the mission field is for the building. Everything in the Christian work must be for the building. This is the Lord's doing. It is a shame to the enemy and a boast to the Lord.

CHAPTER SIXTEEN

THE RECOVERY OF GOD'S BUILDING

(2)

Scripture Reading: Ezra 1:3, 5, 7, 11; 2:1; 3:1-6, 8-13; 4:1-5; 5:1-2

A FULL TYPE OF THE CHURCH

In this message we come to a wonderful point that we call the Lord's recovery. Ezra is a book of recovery, and today we also are in the time of recovery. Whatever is written in the New Testament concerning the church is typified in the Old Testament. In other words, in the Old Testament there is a full type of the church life. Regrettably, however, many Christians today do not pay attention to the type of the church.

Those Christians who do know that the history of Israel is a type of the church apply mainly the things that happened in the beginning of the history of Israel to the Christian life. They know, for example how to apply the Passover and the exodus out of Egypt to the Christian life. They may also know that the crossing of the Red Sea was a type of today's baptism by water, and they know how to apply the eating of manna during the wandering in the wilderness. These are the things that happened at the beginning of the history of Israel. Not many Christians, however, know how to apply to the Christian life the things that happened at the end of the history of Israel. It is not fair to apply only the beginning and not the end of the history of Israel. The entire history of Israel was a full, complete, and entire type of the church life. At the end of the history of Israel there was a captivity, and after the captivity there was the return. Today also is a day of captivity, on the one hand, and of recovery, a return, on the other hand.

At the time of Solomon the temple was built, the glory of God filled the temple, and all the people of Israel were one to worship God. That was wonderful. However, the day of degradation came, and the enemy came from Babylon to destroy the city, burn the temple, capture the people, and carry away all the vessels of the house of God to Babylon. Nebuchadnezzar even put all the things of the worship of God into the idol temple. This was the captivity. Then after seventy years the Lord came in and told the people to go back. The people returned, and after they returned, they rebuilt first the altar and then the temple. This happened in the last part of the history of Israel.

We must look into church history to see what this typifies. The day of Pentecost was the day of glory. The temple in the New Testament, which is the church, was built, and the glory of God filled the church. However, that did not last very long. The day of degradation came in once again, and the church was damaged, destroyed, and scattered into captivity. History tells us that from a certain time captivity after captivity took place, and with captivity there is always the scattering, the divisions. We praise the Lord that at the end time the Lord has come back to recover and to call His people to return to today's Jerusalem. We need to return to rebuild the church, to recover the building of God's house on this earth. By the foregoing simple word we can see the type of the church and its fulfillment. With the history of Israel we have the type, and with the situation of today's church we have the fulfillment.

THE LORD'S NEED FOR A RECOVERY, NOT A REVIVAL

Now we must see what the Lord's recovery is. First we must point out the difference between recovery and revival. We are not speaking here about a revival. A revival is good, even marvelous. However, consider the situation of the people in captivity; even if they had a revival, what good would that have been to the Lord? Perhaps it would have been good for the people, but it would not have been much good for the Lord.

We may illustrate the need for recovery by the scattering in the Old Testament. The city of Jerusalem was in the center of the good land, the temple was built in the center of Jerusalem, and all the people surrounding the temple were one. Then the captivity came in. According to history, the first captivity was to Syria, and later the captivity went to Egypt. In the ultimate captivity almost all the people of Israel were captured to Babylon. By this we can realize that with captivity there is scattering. *Scattering* may not seem to be a negative word, but scattering implies divisions. The people were one in the holy land, but in captivity they were scattered and divided, some to Syria, some to Egypt, and some to Babylon.

While the people were in captivity, some godly ones might have prayed much, asking the Lord to give them a revival. By the Lord's mercy He may have given them a revival there. Considering the whole situation, however, what good would a revival have been to the Lord? Regardless of how many revivals there were and how great they were, the people were still in captivity, and the building of God, the temple, was still destroyed. Even if there were a big revival in Syria, another big revival in Egypt, and many big revivals in Babylon, the Lord might have said, "I do not care for revivals. Regardless of how many revivals you have, I do not have a dwelling place. I do not have a temple. On this earth there is no place for Me to manifest My glory. You may have many revivals, but I am chased away by My enemy from this earth and from My people. You feel very good to have revivals, but I do not care for that. I care for a recovery of the building up of the destroyed temple."

Some have been in Christianity for many years and heard much talk about revival, but they may never have heard about recovery. Many pray, "O God, send us a revival." Many godly ones in the past few centuries did pray very much in this way. Even today some still kneel and pray for a revival, saying, "O Lord, America needs a revival! Oh, send a revival!" After the First World War, many Christian papers were published calling for a revival. I have been reading the newspapers day by day for close to fifty years. I have been watching not only the world situation but also the situation of Christianity. To my observation in all the past forty or fifty years, there has been no real revival. There have been many reports of big healings and other such matters. I went to some of the places where there was such a report. Before I went, there were wonderful reports of revival, but by the time I arrived, the revival was gone. This happened not only in one place but in several places. Today the Lord does not care much for revivals. He cares for a real recovery.

Again I say, if there were revivals in each place of captivity—in Syria, in Egypt, and in Babylon—the Lord would have said, "Regardless of how many revivals you have, I still do not have the temple. Rather, I have shame from the enemy. I do not need a revival. I need the recovery. Rise up and return. For My recovery I need your return. Return from captivity! Return from Babylon! Return back to Jerusalem! This is what I need."

THE RECOVERY BEING WITH
THE SMALL AND LESS SPIRITUAL ONES

We praise the Lord that there was a response to the Lord's call. Not many, but a small number returned to Jerusalem. However, Ezra and Nehemiah, the two books of recovery, tell us that those who returned from captivity were a mess. They were small in number and not very spiritual. They were so timid that only a little opposition caused them to give up the work. Today some among us may be concerned that in the Lord's recovery we are so small. When we hear of opposition, we may be concerned and afraid, and we may want to hide. This is the fulfillment of the type of the recovery. It must be like this; otherwise the type would have no fulfillment. In the type there were the timid and "messed up" ones, and today in the recovery of the church life we also have some timid and "messed up" ones. Hallelujah for this! In a sense there were not many good ones in the recovery. Other than Zerubbabel and Joshua, most were the fearful ones. Therefore, our situation already has been prophesied and typified. When I consider our situation, in one sense I am sorry, but in another sense I am happy. I say, "Praise You, Lord. Here You have the fulfillment of the type." Regardless of how timid the people were, there was still a return, and as long as there was a return there was the recovery.

At that time in Babylon there still were a good number of the people of Israel who were more spiritual and godly. In principle, they may have done the same thing that some dear Christian leaders do today, telling people, "There is no need for you to go to Jerusalem. Just stay here. God is omnipresent; God is everywhere. He is not limited by a place. If God can be there in Jerusalem, to be sure, He can be here with us in Babylon. There is no need to go. Simply be godly and spiritual. God does not care for the place. Babylon or Jerusalem, Jerusalem or Babylon; it is the same. If you are not a spiritual person, regardless of how much you go back to Jerusalem, you will still not be spiritual. If you are a timid person, even if you go back to Jerusalem, you will still be timid."

Do not listen to that kind of message. Consider the return from captivity. Regardless of how timid the people were, regardless of how much they were messed up, they were still the returned captivity. They made it possible for God to have the recovery. Regardless of how spiritual the people in captivity were, they could never rebuild the temple. But regardless of how weak the returned ones were, it was they who rebuilt the temple. They brought in the recovery, and they rebuilt the temple. Today it is the same. Look at the captivity in the Catholic Church, in all the denominations, and even in the small free groups. There is revival after revival, and people are seeking to be spiritual and godly. Some have become spiritual and godly, but where is the rebuilding of the church life? Where is the recovery? Will God be defeated to the uttermost? Do you believe that the Lord Jesus will come back under such a defeated situation? To be sure, He will not. Before His coming back, He has to regain the victory; He has to rebuild the church.

Consider the type, the picture, of the scattering from Jerusalem to Syria, Egypt, and Babylon. This picture is better than a thousand words. After considering this picture, will you still pray for a revival? Will you still seek to be individually spiritual? Will you still seek to be a godly person, merely looking up to the heavens and praying for America and for other places? A spiritual and godly person is wonderful, but consider the picture of the captivity. What can the Lord gain from this kind of person?

Do we believe that in a scattered situation the Lord can come back as the Bridegroom to receive His bride? This would be a shame to Him. If everything among the Christians is poor, yet the Lord comes back in glory as the Bridegroom to receive His bride, Satan will challenge Him, saying, "Jesus, where is Your bride?" The Lord Jesus cannot come back under this kind of situation. Today in this century the nation of Israel has been re-formed, and Jerusalem has been returned. Therefore, today is a day of fast recovery. Jerusalem was returned to Israel, but what about the church? It is still a mess. The Lord must do a quick work to recover the church life!

THE RECOVERY BEING SMALL IN SCALE
BUT RIGHT IN PRINCIPLE

Here we can see a principle. The rebuilt temple was wonderful, but in scale it was smaller than the original one. This was why Ezra tells us that at the time the foundation was laid some were shouting, but some were weeping (Ezra 3:10-13). Some were shouting for joy that the foundation was laid, but some were weeping because of the smaller scale. There was no comparison; the original house was great, but the rebuilt one was smaller. Regardless of the scale, however, the principle is the same. Do not think that in His recovery the Lord will have something great in size, in scale. The Lord will have something small in scale but in the proper principle.

In the church in Jerusalem three thousand were saved in one day and became one. Today we may have only thirty, eighty, or one hundred. However, the principle is the same; we are one. For centuries people have said it is impossible to have oneness among Christians, but today the Lord has worked it out. It is possible. One hundred, two hundred, and even one thousand different Christians among us with different backgrounds are all one.

TODAY'S JERUSALEM BEING OUR HUMAN SPIRIT

We must come back to Jerusalem, but what is today's Jerusalem? First, in the ancient times Jerusalem was the place where God's dwelling place, His habitation, was. Second, Jerusalem was the unique center of the oneness of God's people. It is by Jerusalem that all the people of God were united.

Today's Jerusalem is our human spirit. Ephesians 2:22 tells us that God's dwelling, God's habitation, is in our spirit. Likewise, the genuine oneness is in our spirit. When we are in our mind, we are divided, but when we forget about our mind and return to our spirit, we are one. If you stay in your mind, you are divided from me, and if I stay in my mind, I am divided from you. Therefore, let us forget about our mind and turn to the spirit; then we all will be one. The more we talk and discuss, the more we are in the mind and the more we are divided. Let us forget about discussing. Let us say, "O Lord Jesus." Let us pray and praise together. By doing this, we are immediately in the spirit, and when we are in the spirit, we are one. This shows us that Jerusalem today is our human spirit.

This can also be proved by John 4. In John 4 the Samaritan woman spoke to the Lord Jesus about the place of worship, whether it was in Jerusalem or Samaria, but the Lord Jesus told her that the age had changed. Now worship is not in Jerusalem but in spirit (John 4:19-24). By this we can see that today's Jerusalem is our human spirit. If you come to me to discuss with your mind, we two will be divided. But if we would forget our mind, turn to our spirit, and say, "Amen," we will be one. The more we exercise our mind to argue, the more we are divided. Sometimes I am afraid to talk to certain brothers and sisters, because in talking frankly we may exercise our mind, and after ten minutes we may argue. In the church life we should not talk in this way. Rather, we must learn to say, "O Lord Jesus. Amen." After the meetings when we all arrive home, we should all say, "Amen," in this way. Then everyone will rejoice. Our Jerusalem today is in our spirit, so we must return to our spirit.

The reason why there are differing denominations is that

many people in them are in the mind. Many in the denominations are in the mind, and many in all the different free
groups are also in the mind. Therefore, we should not argue
with them. Argument gets us nowhere. Simply try to touch
the spirit and say, "O Lord," together with them. We should
never try to convince people by our concepts. We cannot convince others in this way. Rather, we must give up our concept
and pray, saying, "O Lord," with people. Help them to turn to
the spirit. This is what we need today.

COMING OUT OF OUR OPINIONS AND TEACHINGS AND BACK TO OUR SPIRIT

Why are we one in the local churches? It is because we give
up mere doctrines and all opinions. In the local churches we
are simply in the spirit. If we are still in the mind, we will be
divided, but now we are in the spirit. We have come back.
Many, however, do not want to come back. Most Christians
prefer to stay in their mind. As long as we stay in the mind,
we are in captivity in the denominations or free groups. If we
are not in the spirit but still in the mind, we are not in Jerusalem. This is pitiful. To be in the mind is to be captured, to be in
captivity. Therefore, we all need to get out of our mind and
turn to our spirit. This is to return from captivity.

By reading some of the books we have published, some
dear ones today have picked up the teaching of the ground of
locality. To them, however, the ground of locality may be something in the mentality. In this way, even the ground of oneness
becomes a divisive factor. The ground of oneness is for oneness, not for division, but if we take the ground of oneness in
our mind and make it a mental matter, right away it becomes
a divisive factor. Instead, we need to return to the spirit.

May the Lord be merciful to us that we all would see what
the difference between revival and recovery is, that today the
Lord needs a recovery, and that the recovery is possible only
in our spirit. We need to drop all kinds of doctrines and all
kinds of opinions. We need to drop not only the wrong doctrines but even the right doctrines and turn to our spirit.
Almost all Christians have some kind of opinion. Some are
for foot-washing, some are for head covering, and some are for

quiet services. Some are for baptism by immersion, while some are for baptism by sprinkling. Some are for this kind of teaching, and some are for that kind of teaching, but as long as we are still in the teachings, we are in the mind, and immediately we are in captivity. We are captured away from the oneness. May the Lord be merciful to us. We need to drop all our teachings, whether foot-washing or head covering. What then shall we do? We should turn to our spirit and say, "O Lord Jesus." To do this is wonderful.

A sister may feel that to play a tambourine is a help to the meeting. If this is merely her opinion, however, she needs to drop it. Many other dear Christians are strict gentlemen and ladies. When they come to the meeting and see brothers with long hair, they shake their head. Rather, they need to shake off their opinion about long hair. I also do not like to see long hair on a brother, but I would not keep this as an opinion. In addition, I do not like to see bare feet; the sisters should cover their feet before they cover their head. However, when I come into the church meeting and see bare feet, I say, "O Lord Jesus." Then I have no problem.

Where could we have the genuine oneness? It is in our spirit. When we turn to the spirit, we are immediately one. We should not say that we like or do not like something. If we say we do not like long hair, the Lord Jesus may say, "I am not bothered." To say this is easy, but we need to realize that we are under a religious concept and a natural makeup; it is truly hard for us to get away from them. Because of this, you have your opinion, and I have my opinion. Then as long as we stay in our mind, we are divided. We need to come back to our spirit; then we are one. We may say that we have left the denominations, but we may not have left all the opinions. We have given up the denominations, but we may not have given up all our teachings. We have left Babylon, but the Babylonian things may still be with us. We need to come out of Babylon and all the Babylonian concepts.

To say this is easy, but to practice this requires the Lord's mercy. We may give up the denominations and come together to practice the church life, but we may do it merely according to doctrine. Yes, we may have left Babylon, the denominations, but none of us may ever have left our opinions, so when we come together we eventually will have difficulties. It is not a matter merely of giving up the denominations. It is a matter of giving up being in our mind. We may give up the denominations but still be in the mind. However, if we give up being in our mind, we will truly come out of the denominations. If we give up being in our mind, all the opinions and mere teachings will be gone.

Over forty years ago, if someone came to me, I would have been strong to check with him as to whether he had been baptized by immersion. If he said yes, I would be happy, but if he said no, I might have turned my back on him. I was strong for baptism by immersion. Then one day I left the denominations, but I still kept this doctrine. After a long time, however, by the Lord's mercy my eyes were opened. Merely to give up the denominations was not good enough. I had to give up the doctrine. We need to come back to Jerusalem, that is, come back to our spirit.

In our mind, we are very complicated, but in our spirit, we are simple. Everyone is simple in their spirit. Elderly people, those over fifty-five years old, are complicated and hard to deal with. However, regardless of a person's education, degree, or age, if he turns to his spirit, he is simple, like a small child. If we mean business with the Lord for His recovery, merely to give up the denominations is not good enough. We need to give up all the teachings, all the opinions, and turn to the spirit. If someone asks, "What about head covering, foot-washing, and baptism?" we should not say much; we should simply say, "O Lord." It would be wonderful if the brothers in a certain place came together and said nothing but, "O Lord." This is the best way to practice the church life.

We are very concerned that a church may be destroyed simply by good opinions. Some may move to a city from several different cities, and some other dear ones may be raised up locally. The ones from one city may say that their former church is the best, and the ones from another city may say that their former church is better than the best. Then those raised up in that city may say their opinion is the best because they were raised up locally. If this happens, that church will be fully destroyed. We must have no opinion. There must be no Chicago, no Akron, no Los Angeles, and no Detroit. There must be only, "O Lord! O Lord!" We need to turn to the spirit. We need a return that the Lord may have the recovery. If we can lay this as a foundation, it is good enough. It is sufficient to practice the church life simply by saying, "O Lord." Try this.

THE NEED FOR THE ALTAR, ALERTNESS, AND THE PROPHETS

The returned ones did not firstly rebuild the temple; they firstly rebuilt the altar (Ezra 3:1-6). In order to have the rebuilding of the church life, we need first to have an absolute consecration. Before building up the church, first set up the altar and put all things on it. This sequence is absolutely right. The altar signifies consecration and absoluteness. The altar means that everything is absolutely for the Lord. Put everything on the altar. The altar is not only for the trespass offering; it is mainly for the burnt offering to be offered morning and evening, daily, continually, and willingly. Before a strong church can be built up in a city, the first thing we must rebuild is the altar. We have to put everything on the altar— what we are, what we do, what we are able to do, what we have, and what we are for. We must be definite and absolute to put everything on the altar, reserving nothing for ourselves.

According to Ezra, they first built the altar and offered on it daily, and then they laid the foundation of the temple (vv. 8-13). When the first temple was built, the people rejoiced when it was completed, but with the rebuilt temple, they did not wait until it was completed. At the time when only the foundation was laid, the people became "crazy." This is because for the rebuilding, the foundation is more important.

After the foundation was laid, the subtle ones came in (4:1-5). Today the situation is the same. We must always be on the alert. Some may come and say that they will help us in the recovery, the rebuilding, of the church. We must be careful to not receive their word too quickly. In Ezra 4, the returned ones told the subtle ones, "You have nothing to do with us in building a house to our God; but we ourselves together will build to Jehovah the God of Israel" (v. 3). Some may say that we are too narrow. It is not that we are narrow; it is that we know the subtlety of the enemy. In Ezra 4, the subtle ones were frustrated.

After laying the foundation, the people did not start right away to build the temple. They needed the prophets to come in to help them (5:1-2). Today in principle it is the same. We need to be absolute and on the alert, and we need the prophets to come in to strengthen us.

THE RECOVERY BEING FOR THE LORD'S GLORY, THE ENEMY'S SHAME, AND OUR FULL SATISFACTION

I look to the Lord that we may see that today is a day not of revival but of recovery. The Lord today does not care much for revival. He cares for the recovery. To be recovered means to come back to the spirit, and to come back to the spirit means to come back to the genuine oneness. We must give up anything that divides. Regardless of how good a teaching, gift, or practice may be, as along as it is divisive, we must drop it and come back to the oneness. The divisions are a shame to the Lord and a boast for the enemy. Today we must drop any kind of divisive factor and come back to the spirit to be one. We do not care for any doctrine, practice, or gift. We care only for the oneness in the spirit. This is the way to have the rebuilding of the Lord's temple. This is the Lord's recovery, and it is a glory to the Lord and a shame to the enemy. This is also our full satisfaction. We have the full satisfaction in our spirit because we realize that we are in the Lord's recovery.

Again I say, today is a day of recovery. What we need is not a revival, but a return to the Lord's recovery. Here and there, in all the big cities in the United States and in all the leading countries on this earth, the Lord will recover His church. This will be a real shame to the enemy, and this will pave the way for the Lord's coming back. When the church is recovered and rebuilt, the Lord will come back with His glory as the Bridegroom to meet the bride. This is a glory to Him and a real and full satisfaction to us.

CHAPTER SEVENTEEN

THE NEW MAN AND THE MAN-CHILD

Scripture Reading: Rev. 2:7, 17, 26-27; 3:12, 20-22; 12:5; 17:3-5; 18:2a, 4; 19:7-9; 22:1-2a, 14, 17

The burden of this chapter can be expressed by the following five phrases: 1) the eternal purpose of God; 2) Adam was the first man; 3) Christ is the second man; 4) the church is the new man; and 5) the overcomers are the man-child.

GOD'S ETERNAL PURPOSE WITH MAN

The First Man

As we saw in chapter one, the eternal purpose of God is to have a corporate man to express Him and represent Him. In order to express God, this man needs God's image, and to represent God, he needs His authority. Genesis 1:26 clearly tells us that God created man in His own image, and He gave man the dominion, the authority, to rule over all things. In order for this man to fulfill God's eternal purpose to express God with His image and to represent God with His authority, this man needs the life of God. Therefore, Genesis 2 presents the tree of life (v. 9).

The first two chapters of the Bible use three important words related to man: *image, dominion,* and *life.* Man was created in the image of God and was committed with God's authority to have dominion over all created things, but he still needed the life of God. God's intention, therefore, was that this corporate man would have His life to live by Him. However, man failed God. He did not take the tree of life but went to the wrong tree, the tree of knowledge. That is, man took knowledge and not God as his life.

In Genesis 2, the tree of life is nothing less than God Himself, and the tree of knowledge is nothing but Satan himself. To take life was to take God, but to take knowledge was to take Satan. The principle today is the same. If we take life, that means we are taking God, but if we take knowledge, we can be sure that we are taking Satan. God is the source of life, while Satan is the embodiment of death. If we take God, we have life. If we take Satan, that is, if we take knowledge, we have death. Knowledge brings death, and by taking knowledge, man failed.

The Second Man

The first man was a failure, but Christ came as the second man. These two terms, *the first man* and *the second man,* are both mentioned in 1 Corinthians 15:45 and 47. The first man failed, but the second man fully succeeded, because the second man, while He was on this earth, day by day and hour after hour constantly took the Father as His life. In John 6:57 Jesus said, "The living Father has sent Me and I live because of the Father." The Son, Jesus, came to live not by Himself but by the Father. He said, "I can do nothing from Myself" (5:30) and "The words that I say to you I do not speak from Myself, but the Father who abides in Me does His works" (14:10). The second man lived by taking God the Father as His life. In this He was successful, but He was only one, an individual. He was the second man but still not the corporate man.

The New Man

God needs a corporate man, a man composed of many men. An individual man alone is not adequate to fulfill God's purpose. Therefore, this second man as a grain of wheat was multiplied. John 12:24 says, "Truly, truly, I say to you, Unless the grain of wheat falls into the ground and dies, it abides alone; but if it dies, it bears much fruit." How can a grain of wheat multiply? There is no other way but to fall into the ground and die. Following death, it grows, and by growing it multiplies. In this way one grain becomes many grains. We are the many grains. Now all the grains are being ground and blended into fine flour in order to make a loaf. First

Corinthians 10:17 says, "Seeing that there is one bread, we who are many are one Body."

This loaf is the new man. The second man has multiplied into the new man. In the Bible there is the first man, the second man, and the new man. The new man is first mentioned in Ephesians 2:15, which says, "Abolishing in His flesh the law of the commandments in ordinances, that He might create the two in Himself into one new man, so making peace." Jesus Christ died on the cross to create a new man of two peoples, the Jewish believers and the Gentile believers. Ephesians 4:24 tells us to put on this new man. To put on the new man simply means that we all have to get into the church life. To put on the new man is to put on the church life. In the church life we are many persons, yet we all are one new man. Moreover, the one new man has one wonderful person, who is Jesus Christ. We are the new man, and He is the person of the new man.

We must never consider that the new man is individual. There is only one new man in the entire universe. No one is a complete new man; we all are simply members of this one new man. The one new man, who is the church, is corporately one.

The Man-child

However, just as the first man failed God, so this new man also failed God. The first man was a failure; the second man was a success, but the new man again became a failure. The last book of the Bible, Revelation, was written after the failure of the new man, that is, after the failure and degradation of the church. This book was written for the purpose of calling the overcomers. As the One who cares for the churches, Christ speaks as the Spirit to the many saints who have become degraded in order to call the overcomers to overcome the degraded situation of the church. These overcomers eventually become a corporate entity which is called the man-child (Rev. 12:5).

BEING UNVEILED TO SEE THE STRATEGIC POINTS
OF THE BIBLE RELATED TO GOD'S ETERNAL PURPOSE

Now we have four titles: the first man, the second man, the new man, and the man-child. Please do not say that this is my teaching. Rather, we should say, "This is the teaching of the Bible." First Corinthians 15:45a speaks of the first man, saying, "So also it is written, 'The first man, Adam, became a living soul.'" Verse 47 mentions the second man: "The first man is out of the earth, earthy; the second man is out of heaven." Then Ephesians 2:15 and 4:24 and Colossians 3:10-11 speak of the new man, who is the church. Finally, Revelation 12:5 speaks of the man-child.

We may have been in Christianity for many years, but we never heard of the first man, the second man, the new man, and the man-child. This shows us the poverty of today's Christianity. These things are clearly revealed and unveiled in the Bible, but we may never have heard them in Christianity. This is a subtlety of the enemy, Satan, because these are the strategic points of the Bible. Christianity has missed these strategic points and turned its attention to the minor, secondary things. Yes, the Bible does tell the wives to submit to their own husband and the husbands to love their wives. However, the Bible is not a book of wives submitting or husbands loving. Do not make the Bible such a book. That is your Bible; that is not God's Bible. The Bible speaks of the eternal purpose of God.

Some may argue with me and say, "Isn't there a verse in the Bible telling wives to submit and husbands to love?" Yes, there is, but there is also a verse that says, "Now the serpent was more crafty than every other animal of the field which Jehovah God had made" (Gen. 3:1). Do you think, therefore, that the Bible is a Bible of the serpent? Do not make the Bible a Bible of the subtle serpent. The Bible also says that a donkey spoke in a human language (Num. 22:28-30). While Balaam, the Gentile prophet, rode on a donkey, all of a sudden that donkey spoke in man's language. Yet, do not make the Bible a Bible of a donkey's speaking. The Bible has many things. The Bible has the serpent, the Bible has scorpions, and the Bible has the lake of fire, but the Bible is not a book of such things. Is the Bible a book of the lake of fire? Is the Bible a book of scorpions? This is foolish, yet it is in this way that Christianity has erred.

Christianity makes the Bible a book of many secondary,

minor things. However, the Bible is a book of God's eternal purpose. God's eternal purpose is not to have a wife submitting to her husband or a husband loving his wife. The Lord Jesus tells us that in the resurrection there will be no more husband and wife (Matt. 22:30). Again, do not argue with me. This is not my teaching; this is the teaching of the Bible. Therefore, do not follow the traditional teaching of Christianity. Come back to the pure Word and remove all your veils.

Many teachings we received from Christianity, whether bad or good, right or wrong, sound or unhealthy, are veils over our eyes. It took me more than fifteen years to take away all these veils. Once when I was in Manila, a dear one came to me and asked, "Brother Lee, why can you see so many wonderful things from the Bible and we cannot?" I told him that was because he had too many layers of veils. Day by day we have the Bible, but we also have not only one layer but many layers of veils on our eyes. We have picked up many doctrines and teachings from our youth until today. Some are good, and some are bad, but they all can become veils.

When the Lord Jesus came to the earth the first time, many publicans, sinners, and Gentiles came to Him, and when they did, they saw something. The Pharisees and priests, however, saw nothing of the Lord because they were veiled with their teachings. The teachings and doctrines they picked up from the Old Testament became their veils. Today it is the same. If I were to go to Mongolia, it would be easy to speak the things of the Lord to the people there. Regrettably, however, it is not as easy to speak in the United States. The Christians here are veiled, covered with all kinds of teachings. If we tell the Mongolians about the second man, they would learn and be glad to know that such a matter is in the Bible. But in this country if I speak of the second man or the man-child, some may accuse me of coming from China with oriental philosophy. This is due to the veils of teachings.

The Bible is not a book of many different matters. The Bible is a book of the eternal purpose of God, which is for God to have a corporate man to express Him with His image and represent Him with His authority by man's taking Him as life. The first man failed God in His purpose, but the Lord

Jesus came as the second man and succeeded. He died and rose again, and in His resurrection He was multiplied. Now we are the many grains blended together to be the new man. However, the majority of the members of this new man failed God again, but the Lord came in to sound out a call, not the first calling but the second calling. The first calling was for our salvation, but now the second calling is for our overcoming. This is not merely to overcome our temper, our little sins, or our little bad habits; it is to overcome degraded Christianity. Those who overcome are the man-child, which eventually fulfills God's eternal purpose. This man-child expresses God and represents God by God's life. This brief word is very simple, but it covers the whole Bible. The entire Bible is under the span of these four men: the first man, the second man, the new man, and the man-child.

THE DEGRADATION OF THE CHURCH

Leaving the First Love toward the Lord

Now we must see how the church as the new man became degraded. According to the first of the seven epistles in Revelation 2 and 3, the church left the first love toward the Lord (2:4). The church turned from the Lord Himself to something that was for the Lord but not the Lord Himself. It turned to works and labor, to do many good things for the Lord (vv. 2-3).

Teachings Bringing in Leaven

Following this, because the church turned from the living, present, and instant Lord Himself to something else, teachings came in. Because someone does many works, he needs the teachings; he labors much, so he needs the knowledge. When the teachings came in, they opened up the door for the subtle one, Satan, to come in. First the good teachings came in, but eventually something corrupting, evil, and ruining was hidden in the teachings. We can see this from the parables in Matthew 13. In Matthew 13 the Lord first came sowing Himself as the seed (vv. 3, 24). This seed grew up as wheat, and from the wheat we have meal, the fine flour (v. 33). Then a woman, that is, the degraded Roman Catholic Church, came in and hid leaven in the meal. By what means did she do this? It was in the way of teachings. Matthew 13:33 says that this evil woman hid leaven in the meal. This means that she picked up many hidden, pagan, and evil things and put them into the fine flour as the hidden leaven.

Revelation 2:20 says that in Thyatira there was the evil woman Jezebel. The Lord Jesus said, "You tolerate the woman Jezebel, she who calls herself a prophetess and teaches and leads My slaves astray to commit fornication and to eat idol sacrifices." The teachings of Jezebel are the teachings with leaven. The Roman Catholic Church teaches people many things. Of what they teach, some things are good, but some things are truly corrupting. In many Roman Catholic cathedrals, for example, there is an image of Jesus. Some may say that the image of Jesus is good, but in the eyes of God it is an idol. I have gone into a number of Catholic cathedrals both in the United States and in Manila. I checked with the people there, asking, "Why do you have this idol here?" They answered, "Do not say this is an idol. This is not an idol; this is our Lord Jesus. Without this image, we can tell people about Jesus, but it is hard for them to apprehend Jesus. If we put an image in the cathedral, right away they can see Jesus. Not only so, they can come here to touch Jesus." This may seem good, but it is a small part of fine flour with a great part of leaven.

When I was in Manila, I found out that some there even changed the Ten Commandments in Exodus 20 in order to fit their situation. They took out the second commandment, which says, "You shall not make for yourself an idol, nor the form of anything that is in heaven above or on the earth beneath or in the water beneath the earth" (v. 4). Then they split one of the other commandments into two in order to fill up the number of ten. This is the subtlety of the enemy, Satan.

Christmas is another item of leaven. How much leaven there is in Christmas! Almost every item of today's celebration of Christmas is pagan. Even the date, December 25, was the day that people in the ancient time worshipped the sun and celebrated its birthday. Moreover, in the ancient time the evergreen tree was related to the worship of idols. All these pagan items in Christmas are related to Satan and to idols. The degraded church, however, says that without such a celebration people cannot appreciate the birth of Christ.

None of us should have a picture of Jesus in our home; that is an idol. The popular picture of Jesus today is a painting of a famous artist in the Middle Ages. However, Jesus did not look like this. Isaiah 53 tell us that while Jesus was in the flesh, He had no beauty; rather, He was despised by people (vv. 2-3). In 1936 in the province of Honan in China we dealt with the case of a sister who was demon-possessed. From our experience we knew that demon possession mostly comes from the worship of idols. Behind any kind of idol there is a demon; if someone has something related to idols in his home, he is in danger of possession by demons. Because in China there are many idol worshippers, I asked the people of that sister's house if they had idols in their home. They said they did not, but eventually I found out that in their home was a picture of Jesus. Later we came to know that the sister many times knelt down to pray to that picture of Jesus. A demon took this opportunity to possess her. I told them to burn that picture, and when they did, the demon left her.

Do not listen to teachings that seem to be good but are leavened. People use a picture of Jesus to help others to appreciate Him. On the one hand, it is good to help people to appreciate Jesus, but there is something subtle there. Leaven is hidden there. The way the church became degraded was first by leaving her direct love to the Lord, taking care of other things which seemed to be good. However, this opened the way for the teachings to come in, and with the teachings leaven came, corrupting, ruining, and leavening the whole church.

Please read Revelation 2 and 3 again. The Lord Jesus mentions teaching several times, but not one mention is positive. He said, "But I have a few things against you, that you have some there who hold the teaching of Balaam....In the same way you also have some who hold in like manner the teaching of the Nicolaitans" (2:14-15). In verse 6 the Lord said that He hates the things of the Nicolaitans. Then in verse 20 He says, "But I have something against you, that you tolerate the woman Jezebel, she who calls herself a prophetess and teaches and leads My slaves astray to commit fornication and to eat idol sacrifices" (v. 20). The Lord Jesus commended "the rest in Thyatira, as many as do not have this teaching" (v. 24). In Revelation 2 and 3, the Lord Jesus hates the teachings.

We should be careful about saying that the Lord Jesus hates only the evil teachings and not the good teachings. How can we know which teachings are good and which teachings are evil? Rather, we should not care for mere teachings. If we do, we will be cheated by them. We must learn to say, "Do not talk to me about mere teachings. I fear them because some are good while others are awful. I may not have the proper discernment, and by the time I find out, I already may have been poisoned." Do not say that this is my opinion or my own teaching. Read these two chapters again and you will see that the Lord Jesus mentions teachings several times, but always negatively.

THE PROMISE OF EATING TO THE OVERCOMERS

On the positive side, the Lord Jesus mentions our eating of Him at least three times. Revelation 2:7 says, "To him who overcomes, to him I will give to eat of the tree of life." This promise of the Lord brings us back to the beginning in Genesis 2. This is the real recovery of the Lord. In the garden of Eden there was no teaching; there was not even a Bible of thirty-nine plus twenty-seven books. What was there at the beginning in the garden was the tree of life.

The overcomers are the ones who overcome all the teachings, who turn from all the teachings to Jesus. The Lord Jesus promised the overcomers to eat of the tree of life. Then He also said, "To him who overcomes, to him I will give of the hidden manna" (Rev. 2:17). The hidden manna is much better than the old manna. The old manna was open to the public, but the Lord gives the hidden manna. It is not public, not open; it is private for the overcomers. Lastly, the Lord Jesus said, "If anyone hears My voice and opens the door, then I will come in to him and dine with him and he with Me" (3:20). To dine is to feast. These verses speak of eating the tree of life, eating the hidden manna, and feasting with the Lord Jesus.

After reading Revelation 2 and 3, will you still be for the teachings? You may say no, but after a short time a certain doctor, a worldwide famous, great speaker, may come to your town. Will you go to hear him? Second Timothy 4:3 says, "For the time will come when they will not tolerate the healthy teaching; but according to their own lusts they will heap up to themselves teachers, having itching ears." This verse speaks not only of one or two teachers but a heap of teachers. This is exactly the situation of today's Christianity. Not many there care for the healthy word. Rather, most like to heap up teachers for their itching ears.

THE SECRET OF OVERCOMING

In what way can we be the overcomers? Clearly, it is by eating. There is no other way. We must not take the way of learning things, the way of picking up teachings. May the Lord be merciful to us that we would pick up this one way, the way of eating Jesus. Day by day we must eat Him as the tree of life, the hidden manna, and the feast. Then we will be the overcomers.

More than forty years ago I read many books about overcoming, and I put the points into practice. I must testify, however, that they did not work. For example, when I was young I was taught that when our temper rises up, we need to reckon that we are dead. I put this into practice not once or twice but many times. However, I found the secret that the more I reckoned I was dead, the more I was alive. Eventually I lost my temper even more. I tried this many times. When I asked others what the problem was, they told me that I was reckoning without faith. That puzzled me very much. No one could tell me what faith is. I spent much time to find out what faith is, but I could not find the definition, and I could not find the way to have faith.

I tried again to reckon myself dead, this time with faith. While I was reckoning, I declared, "I have the faith that I was crucified two thousand years ago." However, after two minutes I lost my temper. Eventually, after more than ten years, by the Lord's mercy I came to know a little what faith is. Faith is nothing less than Jesus. We cannot have faith in ourselves.

Faith is a gift; it is something given by the Lord, and it is the Lord Himself. To be sure, if we have Jesus, we have faith. If we say, "O Lord Jesus! O Lord Jesus!", we will have faith. For many years, I did not have the secret of overcoming my temper, but eventually the Lord gave me the secret. The way to overcome our temper is to call, "O Lord Jesus." Simply breathe Jesus in a little. Jesus is the strongest "chemical agent." When He comes in, right away He neutralizes our anger. Even if we try to lose our temper, we will have no temper. I know this quite well. Previously, the more I reckoned, the more anger I had. But now when the anger comes, I call, "O Lord Jesus," and He neutralizes it; moreover, He turns the anger into praising.

There is no other way to overcome. We do not overcome by holiness. I read many books about holiness. There are different opinions about holiness. According to the teaching of John Wesley, holiness is a sinless perfection. He was absolutely wrong about this. Then those in the "holiness churches" told people to wear certain colors, have dresses of a certain length, and not to paint their faces. At first, I thought they might be right. Then I realized that the rocks on the mountains also do not paint their faces. To not paint one's face is not holiness. Many times I have told sisters who were trying to be holy in this way, "In many Catholic cathedrals there is a statue of Mary. To be sure, if holiness were a proper living, that statue would be very holy. It never loses its temper. It is always quiet and never gets irritated." This is not holiness; this is deadness.

Following this, the Brethren said that holiness is a change of position. In one sense this is right. However, we eventually discovered that our holiness, our sanctification, is Jesus Himself. First Corinthians 1:30 says, "But of Him you are in Christ Jesus, who became wisdom to us from God: both righteousness and sanctification and redemption." Sanctification is something living, shining, and precious. No human word can describe it, because it is Jesus Himself. When we say, "O Lord Jesus" day by day, we eat Him, enjoy Him, and have Him as our holiness. In this way it is difficult to designate what we are, for we become persons who are wonderful. This is the living Jesus as holiness to us.

EATING JESUS BEING OUR ETERNAL PORTION

Now we can see that there is no other way to overcome. The unique way is eating. We need to eat Jesus. Eating is the unique matter in the whole Bible. The Bible starts with the eating of the tree of life, and it ends with the same thing. In the New Jerusalem in the last chapter of the Bible, out of the throne of God flows a river, and on either side of the river grows the tree of life, producing fruits every month to supply the need of all the people of the New Jerusalem.

Revelation 22:14 says, "Blessed are those who wash their robes that they may have right to the tree of life and may enter by the gates into the city." Our eternal right is to eat the tree of life. Many Christians are happy that their robes have been washed, but they do not realize that the washing of the robes is for eating the tree of life. This is our eternal portion and enjoyment.

EATING JESUS BEING THE REVELATION OF THE BIBLE

Jesus is sweet, precious, enjoyable, and available. The day that I came to know that I can eat Jesus, everything changed. The first time I came to this country, in 1958, I was invited to speak to a group in Los Angeles. That was the first time I gave a message in English. My message was on eating Jesus. That was the first time I told people in this country that they need to enjoy Jesus by eating Him. After that message, some persons came to me and said, "Brother Lee, this is a good thought, but we wish to help you to use the proper words to express it." Since this was the first time I had given a message in English, I admitted that I needed some improvement, and I asked them to help me. They said it is better not to use the phrase *eat Jesus*. However, they could not find a better phrase. To eat is simply to eat. What word can we use? Any other word will still mean "to eat." Eventually I told them, "Brothers, do not try to find a better word. The Lord Jesus Himself used this word. In John 6:57 He said, 'He who eats Me, he also shall live because of Me.' This is good enough."

They argued that this is not good English, but no one could find a better English word. This troubling is absolutely due to the old concept. We should not regulate the revelation of the Bible. Rather, our concept needs to be regulated.

Eating Jesus is not my teaching; this is the teaching of the holy Word. The Lord Jesus is our eternal portion not merely for us to learn about but mainly to eat. I have been eating food over sixty-five years. Today, I do not know what vitamin C and vitamin D are; I only know their names. I do not know much about vitamins, but daily I take in many vitamins. We must simply eat Jesus and not care for knowledge.

OVERCOMING BY EATING JESUS

We may be assured that by eating the Lord Jesus we will be overcomers. According to my age, I may be a grandfather, but I am younger than many young people. They are not as living as I am. I am younger than they, not by myself but by Jesus. Jesus is so living! In my speaking some may think that I am "crazy," but in my private room I am more "crazy" with Jesus, because my Jesus is enjoyable. I cannot help myself; I have to be crazy. My Jesus is the living Jesus, not a doctrinal Jesus. My power, my message, and my impact is my enjoyment of Jesus.

We can never return to the old Christianity because our Jesus is too enjoyable. Simply by eating Jesus we will be the overcomers. We will overcome the world, the degraded situation of Christianity, and all the teachings. We will declare, "We do not care for teachings; we only care for our Jesus!"

Yes, I read the Bible, but I do not read it for knowledge; I read it for enjoyment. I may pray-read the beginning of Matthew 1: "Abraham begot Isaac. Amen! Isaac begot Jacob. Amen!" I may not know all about Abraham and Isaac, but oh, the enjoyment I have! The Bible is no more a book of knowledge to me. It is no more a tree of knowledge; it is the tree of life, a book of life, a book of the living Jesus.

By enjoying Jesus in this way, we become the overcomers. Then to be sure, we will try our best to find where there are other Christians like us. We will be anxious to have fellowship with them. This produces the church life, and eventually out of this comes the man-child. By the Lord's mercy, the overcomers are the man-child. We know that the man-child in Revelation 12 is the overcomers because verse 5 says that the man-child will shepherd all the nations with an iron rod. This is similar to 2:26 and 27, which says, "He who overcomes and he who keeps My works until the end, to him I will give authority over the nations; and he will shepherd them with an iron rod." The overcomers are the man-child, and the man-child is the overcomers.

OVERCOMING FOR THE BUILDING

Overcoming to Be Transformed Materials for the Building

The overcomers, who are the eaters of Jesus, are the right materials for God's building. Revelation 2:17 speaks of a white stone with a new name. Years ago I could not understand what this means. Now I realize that this refers to the material for the building. Throughout the Bible stones are material for building. When Simon came to the Lord Jesus, the Lord said, "I also say to you that you are Peter" (Matt. 16:18). *Peter* means "stone." The Lord said that he was no longer Simon but Peter, a stone, for the building up of His church. All the overcomers are white stones with a new name. Their name is new because they have been transformed. At first they were the old clay, but now they are transformed to be a new stone.

Overcoming to Be Pillars in the Temple of God

In Revelation 3:12 the Lord Jesus says, "He who overcomes, him I will make a pillar in the temple of My God, and he shall by no means go out anymore." The overcomers never go out of the temple because they have been built in. They can never pull themselves out again. In principle today, they can pull themselves out from any denomination or any group, but they cannot pull themselves out of the church. The stone is for building, and the pillar is a part of the building. If someone tells me that I am a pillar in the church, I will be happy. Many of the brothers today are the pillars. They can never pull themselves out. Hallelujah, we are the pillars!

Overcoming to Be One with the Lord
and to Be the New Jerusalem

The overcomers are also one with the Lord. Verse 12 continues, "I will write upon him the name of My God and the name of the city of My God, the New Jerusalem, which descends out of heaven from My God, and My new name." The Lord's name will be on us, God's name will be on us, and the New Jerusalem's name will be on us. If I put a label on a brother with his name on it, everyone will know who he is, because he bears a certain name. That the overcomers bear the name of God means that they are one with God. They are men, but they bear the name of God. Are they men, or are they God? They are men who are one with God.

If a man's wife is not one with him, how can she bear his name? If a woman is not Mrs. Jones, she cannot bear the name *Mrs. Jones*. Because she bears such a name, she is Mrs. Jones. The overcomers bear the name of God and bear the name of the new city because they are the new city. If you come to Chicago, you will see a sign that says "Chicago." This city bears the name *Chicago* because it is Chicago. These overcomers will bear the name *New Jerusalem* because they are the New Jerusalem.

The overcomers also bear "My new name," the new name of the Lord. In a sense they are experiencing a new Lord, a new Jesus, a new Christ. Recently I have been condemned for saying that the overcomers in the book of Revelation experience a Christ who is different from the Christ experienced in Christianity. In the Far East someone even rose up to publish a paper condemning me as heretical for saying that the overcomers enjoy a different Christ. Whether or not this is heretical depends on how you interpret it. Yes, we have the same Jesus, but your taste of Him may not be as good as my taste of Him. Even forty years ago Jesus was not as sweet to me as He is today. Today my Jesus is truly a new Jesus. Every day He is new.

To have the new name of the Lord means that we experience something new of the Lord. A brother may have been saved for a few years; is his Jesus exactly the same as He was three years ago? No, He should be much better. This does not mean that he has two "Jesuses." He has the same Jesus, but the taste of Him is new and better.

Overcoming to Be Co-kings with Christ

The overcomers also will be on the throne with Christ as His co-kings (2:26-27; 3:21). Christ is on the throne, and they also will be on the throne. He has the power and authority, and they also will have the same power and authority to rule over the nations.

Overcoming to Be the Bride of Christ

As we have seen, the overcomers are the man-child to fulfill God's eternal purpose. Eventually, this man-child will be the bride to satisfy Christ (19:7-9). To the enemy and to fulfill God's purpose we are the man-child, while to satisfy Christ we are His bride. In Revelation 17 Babylon the Great is the great harlot and the mother of harlots (vv. 1, 5). No overcomer should stay in today's Christianity. Apostate Christianity is not the bride; it is the harlot, either the mother harlot or the daughter harlots. The Lord says to those in Babylon, "Come out of her, My people" (18:4).

The way to be the overcomers is to eat Jesus. By eating we have growth and transformation, and we are good for God's building. We are something new, and we have new experiences of God and of the Lord. Then we will be the overcomers, the man-child, and eventually the bride to satisfy Christ.

ABOUT THE AUTHOR

Witness Lee was born in 1905 in northern China and raised in a Christian family. At age 19 he was fully captured for Christ and immediately consecrated himself to preach the gospel for the rest of his life. Early in his service, he met Watchman Nee, a renowned preacher, teacher, and writer. Witness Lee labored together with Watchman Nee under his direction. In 1934 Watchman Nee entrusted Witness Lee with the responsibility for his publication operation, called the Shanghai Gospel Bookroom.

Prior to the Communist takeover in 1949, Witness Lee was sent by Watchman Nee and his other co-workers to Taiwan to ensure that the things delivered to them by the Lord would not be lost. Watchman Nee instructed Witness Lee to continue the former's publishing operation abroad as the Taiwan Gospel Bookroom, which has been publicly recognized as the publisher of Watchman Nee's works outside China. Witness Lee's work in Taiwan manifested the Lord's abundant blessing. From a mere 350 believers, newly fled from the mainland, the churches in Taiwan grew to 20,000 in five years.

In 1962 Witness Lee felt led of the Lord to come to the United States, settling in California. During his 35 years of service in the U.S., he ministered in weekly meetings and weekend conferences, delivering several thousand spoken messages. Much of his speaking has since been published as over 400 titles. Many of these have been translated into over fourteen languages. He gave his last public conference in February 1997 at the age of 91.

He leaves behind a prolific presentation of the truth in the Bible. His major work, *Life-study of the Bible,* comprises over 25,000 pages of commentary on every book of the Bible from the perspective of the believers' enjoyment and experience of God's divine life in Christ through the Holy Spirit. Witness Lee was the chief editor of a new translation of the New Testament into Chinese called the Recovery Version and directed the translation of the same into English. The Recovery Version also appears in a number of other languages. He provided an extensive body of footnotes, outlines, and spiritual cross references. A radio broadcast of his messages can be heard on Christian radio stations in the United States. In 1965 Witness Lee founded Living Stream Ministry, a non-profit corporation, located in Anaheim, California, which officially presents his and Watchman Nee's ministry.

Witness Lee's ministry emphasizes the experience of Christ as life and the practical oneness of the believers as the Body of Christ. Stressing the importance of attending to both these matters, he led the churches under his care to grow in Christian life and function. He was unbending in his conviction that God's goal is not narrow sectarianism but the Body of Christ. In time, believers began to meet simply as the church in their localities in response to this conviction. In recent years a number of new churches have been raised up in Russia and in many eastern European countries.